straight talk

Clear Answers about Today's Christianity

Jerry Pattengale

with J. Bradley Garner and Lisa Velthouse

Triangle Publishing
Marion, Indiana

Straight Talk: Clear Answers about Today's Christianity
Jerry Pattengale with J. Bradley Garner and Lisa Velthouse

Second Edition

Direct correspondence and permission requests to one of the following:
E-mail: info@trianglepublishing.com
Web site: www.trianglepublishing.com
Mail: Triangle Publishing
1900 West 50th Street
Marion, Indiana 46953
USA

Pattengale, Jerry with J. Bradley Garner and Lisa Velthouse
Straight Talk: Clear Answers about Today's Christianity

Second Edition

ISBN: 978-1-931283-27-4

Illustrator: Ron Mazellan
Cover design: Jim Pardew
Graphic design: Lyn Rayn
Photographs: Courtesy of Integrity Design Studio

Printed in the United States of America

this book is dedicated

to the memory of

David E. Tiller (1957–1989)

He was full of life and lives on in Jason, Joshua, and Nicholas,
my three oldest sons. I have not met a person from his life that
doesn't miss him, and I look forward to introductions
in heaven—where his smile will last forever.

and to the memory of

Scott Knupp (1962–1979) and Tom Knupp (1965–1983)

Like David, their short lives were full and friendships many, and God is
enjoying their fellowship. Their moving teenage testimonies have inspired
many of us, and their father and mother, Carl and Myrna, have
become dear friends and special surrogate parents.

Jerry Pattengale, 2004

contents

preface

My introduction to college was memorable. I was a brand-new Christian at a "Christian college." Instead of attending the big state school, I switched late in the summer on advice from my new Christian friends. After the first couple of days of fun and orientation activities, the big meeting with my adviser took place—and my introduction to the academic side was about to reveal just how much I needed to learn.

My adviser already was a legend. He had led dozens of trips to Israel, was a self-made millionaire from smart and frugal real estate investments, served as the campus chaplain, was among the most popular professors on campus, and even attracted a quarter of the student body to a 10 PM weekly share time.

In contrast, I had visited college campuses only a few times in the past and then only briefly. Before this week, I was acquainted with very few college students. Suddenly, I was standing in the basement of a dark building in the presence of a famous professor.

Trying to disguise my nervousness, I pointed to the oversized historic portrait behind the large worn wooden desk of Dr. Wilbur Williams and said conversationally, "That's a great picture. Is that your great-grandmother?"

He looked up at me and, for a moment, time stood still. In a voice that echoed through the halls of the gloomy basement into the shadowed corridors of the distant past, a voice undoubtedly borrowed from God, he replied, "That, young man, is John Wesley."

To understand the significance of this event, you need to see the context in which it took place. Dr. Williams and I were in a basement room of the original College Wesleyan Church, long since converted to the Religion Department on what is now the campus of Indiana Wesleyan University. At that time, the international headquarters of The Wesleyan Church also was located nearby.

I wasn't even clear what Christianity was all about, let alone why there were so many denominations like the Wesleyans and Methodists. Although a high school graduate, I didn't understand the differences between Catholics and Protestants, Moonies and Mormons, or why some people were called "evangelicals" or "fundamentalists."

My introduction to John Wesley and the movement carrying his name was a bit awkward, and remains a vivid memory. Thirty years later, I'm back on the same campus—and my office window provides a clear view of a striking ten-foot-tall bronze statue of this famous religious leader.

During the past three decades, I've learned that a host of great men and women have led noble Christian causes. They have helped throngs of people develop a meaningful relationship with Christ and attain a reasonable understanding of the biblical message. I've also learned that what this amazing group of religious leaders has in common is what is central to the Christian message—its basic orthodox (or straight) teachings.

Straight Talk is arranged in a user-friendly format to help you navigate and more fully understand Christianity's basic teachings. The introduction that follows is intended to give you the rationale for the book's format and its focus on the questions people commonly ask about Christianity.

Perhaps you already have found books by Christian writers and leaders helpful in understanding how some key doctrines influence other teachings and life applications. C. S. Lewis, Charles Spurgeon, John Calvin, Billy Graham, Ravi Zacharias, John Wesley, Mother

Teresa, and a host of others offer some wonderful insights and systems of theology. However, these books, like *Straight Talk*, should be considered secondary sources.

Straight Talk's purpose is to bring key doctrines to the surface—those taught by Christ through His own words and in those of His disciples—using the Bible as the primary source. In the future, no matter whether you find a writer brilliant or bland, you'll have a collection of the key doctrines along with some exercises that help to unpack them.

As you start through the introduction, and then as you jump into the chapters and the key concepts, I hope that the journey is less awkward than my basement introduction to Christianity. Imagine yourself sitting at that large worn wooden desk. Instead of an oversized historic portrait of Wesley, a picture of Jesus Christ hangs behind you on the wall. How would you answer if one of your friends walked into the room and asked, "Who is that?" How would you respond if your friend's next question was, "Why do you have it in your office?" What if your friend asked, "Can you tell me in a nutshell what He believed?" Could you do that?

Well, this text is designed to help you with these queries and to serve as a reference for future questions.

First, it's your turn to stand in front of the desk.

It's important to make sure that the picture in the frame matches the picture in print.

Jerry Pattengale
July 2007

acknowledgments

This book's genesis stretches back nearly fifteen years, with the first draft of the glossary written at Scripps' Dennison Library in Claremont, California—one of our country's finest places to reflect and write. Thanks to the Dennison staff and to the accommodating students at the nearby *Motley Café* for listening to a writer think out loud, and for introducing me to frozen cookie dough long before it was fashionable.

Terry Franson, Mike Schoonover, and David Weeks were all supportive in their own ways during the early days of writing, and the students at Azusa Pacific University were helpful with feedback.

A special thanks goes to the group that helped me bring years of thoughts and notes together with new material into this *Straight Talk* text. I salute the thousands of first-year students at Indiana Wesleyan University who provided four years of surveys and solicited comments—and who selected the book's cover. And to Bayard "By" Baylis for his relentless support as both a colleague and veteran author.

The co-authors of *Straight Talk* were wonderful. J. Bradley Garner gave special assistance with the object lessons and interactive sections—in short, he helped turn the manuscript into a user-friendly text. Lisa Velthouse added wonderful concluding reflections and graced the book with her talent. Ron Mazellan, a New York Times

Best-Seller illustrator (2007), added his strokes of genius through the illustrations. The picture opening chapter one has been requested for other books, and a four-foot copy hangs in the Center for Life Calling and Leadership at Indiana Wesleyan University—a framed expression of the university's commitment to helping students find their life purpose.

Clarence "Bud" Bence served as a reader and co-authored the early work. In a book like this, it was especially helpful to have a veteran theologian's feedback.

Two special writing soul mates, whose candid comments and soft suggestions helped with clarity, have become good friends. It's hard to separate their help on this and other texts as grammar and metaphoric questions flew back and forth. These two writers, both with many years in Gannett's editing world, are Mike Cline and Alan Miller.

My wife Cindy tolerated many readings and drafts, along with our sons Michael, Nick, Josh, and Jason. Their comments are always appreciated. My siblings continue to help fill the gaps in the stories from Buck Creek, some of which appear in the chapter introductions. Thanks to Victoria, Vivian, Veronica, Vincent, Orval, Virginia, and Abraham, my mother and to our ninety-five-year-old grandpa, Ralph Saubert, for indulging so many questions.

The main support for *Straight Talk* came from the staff at Triangle Publishing. Aimee Williams edited the first draft. Besides doing a wonderful job of smoothing sentences, she saved me from printing some hilarious mistakes. Lyn Rayn's graphic design adds much to the manuscript's visual appeal. Editor Bobbie Sease fine-tuned the formatted drafts unobtrusively but with class. A deep thanks to these talented new friends and to the publisher, Nathan Birky, for pushing along the project in an expeditious manner.

The individuals above have helped with this book, for which I'm grateful. But I also lift my eyes higher to give thanks to God, whose sustaining grace assisted not only with this book, but with all the chapters of my life—those written and those still in process.

Jerry Pattengale
Revised July 2007

introduction

straight talk

*And the things you have heard me say in the presence
of many witnesses entrust to reliable men who will
also be qualified to teach others.*
(2 Timothy 2:2)

straight talk

We hear conflicting messages about Christ from such a wide variety of sources. Before becoming a Christian, I sat at a dingy coffeehouse listening to a group of mullet-headed Christian rockers sing "Jesus Is Just All Right With Me" and "Stairway To Heaven." Then they sang "My Sweet Lord" by George Harrison—one of the Beatles who had become a pronounced follower of Hare Krishna. I'm not the sharpest knife in the drawer, but figured out that the no-name group was a bit misguided. I was hearing bizarre interpretations of the message of Christ—by rockers who selected the songs to convert us longhairs sitting at the old wooden wire spool tables in front of them. When they paused for a quick plug about their Lord, and asked us to bow "with nobody looking around," I looked around. Across the room were flickering orange globes surrounded by a few hippies. Many were smiling back at me. One suede-vested, bare-chested ragamuffin raised his *RC* as a toast. When asked if we wanted "to accept the Lord as our Savior?" I whispered to my date, "Would that be Krishna?"

If you're like me, seeing the names of religious books, movies, musicians and other sources brings instant images, and endorsement or caution. *Blue Like Jazz.* Big Daddy Weave. *Godspell.* David Robinson. *Jesus Christ Superstar. The Jesus I Never Knew.* John Maxwell. *The Last Temptation of Christ. The Mission. The Witness.* The *JESUS* Film. Robert Duvall's *The Apostle.* Steve Martin's *Leap of Faith.* Jimmy Swaggart. Michelangelo's *Pietà.* Billy Graham. *The Crucible. The Robe.* Handel's *Messiah.* Jim Bakker. Amy Grant. Reggie White. Deion Sanders. *Oh, God.* The Newsboys. The W's. Supertones. *"Jesus is Just All Right With Me."* The Power Team. Dr. James Dobson. Chuck Colson. Chuck Swindoll. Moonies. Mormons. Baptists. Quakers. Wesleyans. Methodists. *The Discovery Channel.* Your saintly old neighbor. *The Scarlet Letter.* Internet chats, blogs, and Web pages. *Candide. My Name is Asher Lev.* The Columbine teens who died for their faith in God. *K-Pax.* C. S. Lewis. *The DaVinci Code, The Passion of the Christ.*

And what's up with the John 3:16 fan who sports the bizarre rainbow-colored Afro? Or the huge tattooed crosses on NBA players? *Touched by an Angel*? Those Amish carriages? *The Purpose-Driven Life?* That *B.C.* cartoon? Or . . . ?

"Who has the right message?" Or more importantly, "What is the truth about Jesus and the religion He founded called Christianity?"

Most people have heard numerous discussions, lectures, sermons, and/or jokes about Christ and Christianity. And I assume you have read about Him or His followers as well—both the famous and the infamous. Quite possibly, you have listened to music or watched movies written by Christians, maybe some listed above. Or, you have read creative poetry and fiction about Christ and related topics, such as heaven. If you haven't heard the song "I Can Only Imagine" by Mercy Me, listen sometime and see if it provokes you to think about heaven—regardless of what you know about it.

Bumper stickers, plastic fish, dove symbols, press interviews, and editorials parade before us an endless assortment of statements about Christianity—often contradictory, sometimes appealing, at times provocative, other times irritating. But whatever questions these symbols and messages raise, we at least will answer one very basic question: "Do I believe in Christ?" Yes, we all answer, either by design or default. The aggressive parade of reminders, these and a thousand more, prompt and beg this question. Not answering it is a conscious decision not to believe.

If Christ, Satan, heaven, and hell are indeed realities, which I believe them to be, ignoring such issues will by no means lessen their importance. One's rejection of the truth does not negate that truth.

As a historian, the reality of past events and personalities consumes much of my time. I am constantly checking primary sources to verify the validity of statements made by my students and by various scholars. For example, I recently graded a paper on Platonism (Plato's beliefs), and could only ascertain the accuracy of the paper by consulting the *Republic* (Plato's main work), not another researcher's analysis. Nothing short of studying the primary source would suffice. Should not the same principle apply to one's inquiry into Christianity? Most certainly.

In order to gain an informed opinion about Christianity, we need to consult its primary source—the Bible. Although students may need the assistance of a professor to understand Plato, they should, in turn, evaluate for themselves any commentary on Platonism against the very words of Plato. Likewise, all discussions on Christianity should be measured against the very words of Christ.

As a historian, I also realize that to know Christ's words, to read and study them, and to know about His life, death and Resurrection is to know history. But to accept these words as truth, to place faith in Christ as Lord and the giver of eternal life, is quite a different matter.

It is salvation.

The following text is written for the person who desires to understand Christ, based on His central teachings, not mullet-headed or gray-haired representations. Although my colleagues and I try to provide helpful context for Christ's teachings, keep in mind that the primary source—the actual Scriptures—are your best reference. Christ's central teachings are the basis for each chapter, the foundation upon which my commentary stands.

During the 1970s, people often assumed that my long hair meant my mind was asleep and my heart was cold. That's not what Christ thought. I know—I read His words for myself. I challenge you to do the same.

Jerry A. Pattengale
Marion, Indiana Revised July 2007
Listening to Big Daddy Weave

about this book

What is Christianity? In the light of conflicting views, this is a timely and important question. A T-shirt slogan or creative story doesn't answer this question. Neither does a film based on a moving story of hope, or a powerful song about heaven. These pieces of information might help, but are secondary sources at best. We come back to the primary question, "What is Christianity?" Could you answer this question if asked in a class? Could you blog intelligibly about it, or recognize erroneous comments in chat rooms?

In its simplest form, Christianity is a religion based on the doctrines and teachings of Jesus Christ, a historical figure also referred to as Christ, Lord, Messiah, and Savior. His words are recorded in Christianity's primary source: the New Testament of the Bible. All of the New Testament writers had direct contact with Jesus or His disciples, and also held to the validity and importance of the Old Testament. Because Christ had personally inspired these writings, the New Testament books are unique among all writings about Him and Christianity.

After placing their faith in Jesus, some of His followers wrote down His essential teachings and recorded many of His actions. We have copies of their writings in the form of ancient manuscripts, dating to within a generation of Christ's death, ca. AD 33. Fortunately, scholars have gone back to these ancient manuscripts and translated them into modern languages. In other words, when you read the New Testament you are reading a translation of the very words of Jesus upon which the New Testament authors made their personal decisions of faith. Some liberal scholars assert that the "exact" words of Christ were lost in translation. Even if that were the case, the essence of His teachings remains intact. You have the privilege of reading Christ's teachings for yourself and making your own choice.

Ultimately, one joins the ranks of Christianity—becomes a Christian—through faith. This faith is not in scientific research, archaeology, ancient manuscripts, or the opinions of scholars on the validity of the New Testament. Although these sources are valuable and can prove helpful, one does not become a Christian by putting faith in them. Rather, one becomes a Christian by making a personal commitment to Jesus Christ, believing that He is the divine Son of God, accepting His free grace-given gift of salvation and the forgiveness of sins, and endeavoring to follow His teachings.

Remember, if you choose not to follow Jesus Christ, your choice does not nullify the fact of His existence in history, the authenticity of His statements, and the record of His promises. An analysis of the biblical record reveals over 40 prophecies that were made and fulfilled by the birth, death, and resurrection of Jesus Christ. You choose then, either by design or by

A Dollar, a Blind Man, and the State of Texas

What are the odds of one man fulfilling all of the predictions of time, place, and circumstances of the Messiah? We asked a mathematician. Here's an illustration with the same odds. Cover the State of Texas, all 267,339 square miles of it, with silver dollars three feet high. This would be almost 7.5 trillion cubic feet of silver dollars. Mark one of those silver dollars with an X and throw it somewhere in the pile. Now drop a man blindfolded from an airplane over Texas, and tell him to reach down, anywhere, and pick one silver dollar. The odds of him picking the dollar with the X are the same as one man satisfying all of the predictions of the Messiah. But that is exactly what Christ did (fulfilled the predictions, that is; not the dollar thing).

Bruce Bickel and Stan Jantz
Bruce and Stan's Guide to God[1]

default, to put your faith in something else. And if you do choose to follow Christ, to become a Christian—"saved" and brought into a personal relationship with Jesus Christ—your choice is one based on faith in the unseen, the supernatural. You may have been influenced by the counsel of others or the mass of archaeological and historical evidence supporting the authenticity of the Bible. But, according to the very words of Christ Himself, one chooses to follow Him and His teachings, not simply interpretations or supporting evidence. This is entirely an act of faith. Other things may support your decision, but His promises are the basis for eternal hope and true inner peace.

This text has been designed to provide the reader with an opportunity to interact with the timeless truths of Christianity. With this outcome in mind, readers are given the challenge to think, reflect, and, perhaps, grapple with what they believe. The material in each chapter is organized into the following sections:

Consider the Source

Each chapter opens with several key scriptural references that frame the focus and content. We strongly intend to focus our attention on the source for all truth, God's Holy Word, the Bible. Through this process, the reader will be able to make direct connections between the topic of discussion and God's promises and commands for His people.

Understand the Need

This section of the text provides analysis and clarification of the issue being discussed. Additionally, it provides the reader with a means for making personal connections between the biblical text and one's personal spiritual walk.

FAQ

A number of "Frequently Asked Questions" (FAQ) arise from discussions and examination of God's Word. In this section of the text, we provide some answers to questions that college students frequently ask as they engage the Scriptures.

Reaction and Reflection

A key component of your experience with this text will be time that you invest in "Reaction and Reflection" (R&R). This time provides you with the opportunity to pray, digest what you are learning, seek additional information from other resources, make personal applications of the content, and listen to what God is saying to you.

Style Notes

Unless otherwise noted, all New Testament references used in this text are from the New International Version (NIV) of the Bible. This is one of the most accurate translations available, taken directly from the oldest available copies of the Old and New Testaments. Several translations or versions of the Bible exist, but not all were derived from the oldest manuscripts. Some of these translations are weak, altering the meaning of the original text or using inconsistent word meanings. Other translations use an awkward prose that is difficult for most people to read and understand. The NIV is the product of a comprehensive group of established scholars from various religious backgrounds. It is popular among both scholars and churches today. For clarification of common words used in the Christian community, consult the glossary. Additionally, the first occurrence of terms appearing in the glossary are *italicized*.

Reaction and Reflection

Over the next several weeks, you will be provided with an opportunity to explore and examine some of the key elements of your faith and the nature of your relationship with Jesus Christ. As John Wesley observed, "We are always open to instruction, willing to be wiser every day than we were before, and to change whatever we can change for the better."[2] This open, vibrant expectation to be a lifelong learner will enhance your faith and your ability to impact your world for Christ.

We are praying that this will be a time of reflection and insight. Each chapter contains a series of questions and activities designed to assist you in processing information and personalizing it to your life experience. We strongly suggest that you begin each "Reaction and Reflection" session with a time of prayer, seeking God's guidance and direction as you think and respond. One additional suggestion is that you find a partner with whom you can share and discuss your responses. As we are told in God's Word:

> *And let us consider how we may spur one another on toward love and good deeds. Let us not give up meeting together, as some are in the habit of doing, but let us encourage one another—and all the more as you see the Day approaching.* (Hebrews 10:24–25)

Sharing this experience with a trusted friend provides opportunities for mutual encouragement and accountability. Our spiritual growth is often enhanced and accelerated as we interact with fellow travelers who share our faith on the journey of life.

1. How would you describe the nature of your relationship with God?

2. Which areas of your spiritual life do you feel are the strongest?

3. Which areas of your spiritual life may be in need of some encouragement, support, or additional information? (We all have these areas of need in our lives.)

4. What are some faith questions you hope to answer as you proceed through this study?

Endnotes

1. Bruce Bickel and Stan Jantz, *Bruce and Stan's Guide to God: A User-Friendly Approach* (Eugene, OR: Harvest House Publishers, 1997), 175.

2. Holland N. McTyeire, *A History of Methodism* (Nashville: Publishing House of the Methodist Episcopal Church, 1892), 203.

understanding the basics

doctrinal positions and principles

*For where your treasure is, there
your heart will be also.*
(Matthew 6:21)

a college moment:
waking up with answers

When I noticed my college friend asleep in our theology class, the temptation was too, well . . . tempting. I nudged him on his shoulder and whispered, "Paul, Paul, Dr. Haines is calling on you."

With seismic force the stocky napper bolted to his feet. His large quads thrust the metal desk forward on the faded basement tile—a screeching lecture stopper. Professor Haines was standing in the aisle only a few seats away with a textbook in hand, held open with his thumb.

Time stood still, yet the moment passed all too quickly. Our prof was visibly shaken and in disbelief. He gazed at this young disheveled groggy student with cockeyed glasses and a shirt that could pass for a topographical map. Dr. Haines, who had been mid-sentence on the topic of the Trinity, had little chance to respond. Paul blurted out, "Dr. Haines, sir . . . uh, sorry, sir. I had the answer on the tip of my tongue and lost it."

The brilliant professor gathered his wits, looked sternly at the novice theologian, and rebuked him. "Young man," scolded Dr. Haines, "this is the saddest day in my teaching career. Scholars have been looking for the answer to the Trinity for centuries—and you had it on the tip of your tongue and lost it! Now sit down and be quiet."

Although not all biblical beliefs are as hard to grasp, nor learning experiences as memorable, it can take considerable work to come to a reasonable understanding of some of the Bible's key teachings. When the above story took place, I was a new Christian and had only recently learned the difference between the Old and New Testaments. Terms like "Trinity" and "theology" were not in my high school vocabulary. Even the main creed of Christianity, the "Nicene Creed," was new to me.

This first chapter unpacks a few of these central teachings of Christianity. Like the remaining chapters, all key teachings are founded directly on biblical statements, to which references are given. The creeds show the need for the early Christians to summarize key documents in order to determine which churches were abiding by biblical standards.

There are still times when I think I have answers, but they elude me. However, through categorizing key questions and highlighting key Scriptures, those times are less frequent. Likewise, I hope the chapter's format helps to bring clarity to some foundational Christian teachings and historical developments.

understanding
the basics

doctrinal positions and principles

 ## Consider the Source

Yet for us there is but one God, the Father, from whom all things came and for whom we live; and there is but one Lord, Jesus Christ, through whom all things came and through whom we live. (1 Corinthians 8:6)

For we were all baptized by one Spirit into one body— whether Jews or Greeks, slave or free—and we were all given the one Spirit to drink. (1 Corinthians 12:13)

In these passages the Apostle Paul identifies several essential Christian beliefs or doctrines. His audience is a group of people known as the Corinthians, who were notorious for their worship of heathen idols. In communicating with the Corinthians, Paul found it necessary to present a concise statement that distinguished Christian teachings from those associated with idols, or man-made gods. Note his claims:

- A belief in one God (monotheism) as opposed to many gods (polytheism)

- A belief in one Christ, the Son of God, yet fully His equal; together They created everything that is
- A belief in the Holy Spirit, the presence of God here on earth

Later, Christians would term these three—God the Father, Jesus Christ the Son, and the Holy Spirit—as the Trinity. Paul's assertions accurately reflect Christ's teachings and correspond with the rest of the biblical writers. In this chapter, we will explore these and other aspects of church doctrine and provide you with a framework for examining your own faith and beliefs in a number of critical areas.

Understand the Need

How would you respond if one of your best friends asked you the following question: "What do Christians believe, anyway?" On the surface, that seems like a harmless and simple question. Yet for many people who profess to be Christians, that question may present some clear challenges primarily related to at least three possible scenarios:

1. The individual may have a lack of knowledge and understanding as to the exact nature of his or her doctrinal beliefs (and difficulty in describing what Christians believe).

2. Doctrinal beliefs are often viewed as fluid, flexible, and subject to change based upon the demands and influences of the culture (an individual might have difficulty maintaining Christian beliefs in the midst of challenge).

3. Without a firm set of beliefs and an understanding of the biblical basis for those beliefs, Christians may be vulnerable to the influence of articulate communicators, and to assertive groups that espouse positions and doctrines that are suspect (leaving the Christian susceptible to false teachings about the Christian faith) when compared to the actual Bible.

In each of these situations, a viable solution is for Christians to have sufficient knowledge and understanding of what they believe in order to present a logical and coherent response based upon sound biblical principles and teachings.

Understanding Church Doctrine

There are literally hundreds of varieties of Christian denominations. Each of these denominations is grounded on a specific set of beliefs related to an interpretation of the Bible. The followers of these denominations presumably have some level of knowledge and understanding of the doctrinal distinctives that differentiate their chosen denomination from others in the Christian faith. Christians tend to spend a great deal of energy distinguishing their own denominational beliefs from those of others. Quite often, however, they do not have a full enough grasp of their own beliefs to make those kinds of comparisons.

We would suggest that an overwhelming majority of Christians need to spend more energy learning about the doctrinal details of the faith—what we believe and why we believe it. As a means of facilitating some understanding of the slippery slope of denominational belief, church researcher George Barna proposed that the American culture can be divided into five "faith-based segments":

- **Individuals who are "born again"** (people who profess a personal commitment to Jesus Christ that is important in their lives, and who believe that when they die they will go to heaven because they have confessed their sins and accepted Jesus Christ as their Savior)
- **Individuals who are "evangelicals"** (born-again Christians who additionally believe that they have a responsibility to share their faith with others, that their faith is very important in their lives, that God is a real being who is all-knowing and all-powerful, and that the Bible is totally accurate in what it teaches)
- **Individuals who are Christians but are not born again or evangelical** (in Barna's terms, "notional Christians")

- **Individuals who are atheists and agnostics** (those who deny the existence of God)
- **Individuals who identify with a faith other than Christianity**[1]

The percentages of Americans who identify with each of these groups is as follows: born-again Christians (33%), evangelical Christians (8%), notional Christians (44%), atheists and agnostics (8%), and faith groups other than Christianity (7%).[2] Based upon these descriptions, how would you describe the nature of your faith?

From a different perspective, theologian Richard Foster has proposed the concept of six varied traditions of the Christian faith:

- **The Contemplative Tradition** (focus on prayer, meditation, and spiritual reading)
- **The Holiness Tradition** (a focus against sin in favor of acts of love and mercy)
- **The Charismatic Tradition** (welcoming the Holy Spirit and exercising the gifts while living in the joy and power of the Spirit)
- **The Social Justice Tradition** (serving others and working for justice in all human relationships)
- **The Evangelical Tradition** (sharing one's faith with others as God leads)
- **The Incarnational Tradition** (seeking to show the presence of God in all that one does)[3]

In reviewing this list of categories provided by Barna, readers are probably able to identify several that would apply to the focus of their faith lives or as an emphasis of their chosen denominations. In regard to denominational theology, it is probable that most denominations, although they may lean predominantly to one of these categories, could also be reasonably associated with multiple categories. These categories merely serve to provide a template for thinking about doctrine in relation to biblical truths.

Understanding and interpreting the truths of God's Word is no simple task, but is one that we all should be pursuing with enthusiasm. In an analysis of the techniques and approaches to hermeneutics (the science of interpreting an author's meaning), Grant Osborne made the following observations in regard to hermeneutics and biblical text:

> The hermeneutical enterprise . . . has three levels . . . We begin with a third-person approach, asking "what it meant" (exegesis); then passing on to a first-person approach, querying "what it means for me" (devotional); and finally taking a second-person approach, seeking "how to share with you what it meant to me" (sermonic).[4]

Although this observation does add direction and multiple purposes to our quest for what God means to communicate to us through His Word, the question remains, "Yes, but how?" Unfortunately, there is no easy answer to this question. If you don't believe us, take a trip to the library and examine the vast assortment of biblical commentaries that endeavor to find and describe the meanings of the biblical text. It is well beyond the scope of this text to elaborate strategies for the hermeneutical enterprise. It is, however, reasonable to consider the dimensions of biblical understanding that contribute to the formulation of church doctrine.

One of the key means for understanding church doctrine is to strive continually to increase both knowledge and understanding of God's Word. By this endeavor, we should be able to: (1) articulate the various features and emphases of doctrine, (2) identify false teachings that are counter to biblical truths, (3) describe/defend the features of our faith, and (4) live in accordance to those doctrinal beliefs. In other words, we must always give first consideration to the source and we must always seek to verify and understand church doctrine as it relates to the original source for all doctrine. The Navigators, an organization that promotes strategies for ongoing spiritual growth and biblical living, propose the following strategies to help us continually increase our biblical knowledge:[5]

- **Hear God's Word**

Hearing the Word from godly pastors and teachers provides insight into others' study of the Scriptures, and stimulates one's own appetite for the Word.

Consequently, faith comes from hearing the message, and the message is heard through the word of Christ. (Romans 10:17)

- **Read God's Word**

Reading the Bible gives an overall picture of God's Word. Many people find it helpful to use a daily reading program to take them systematically through the Bible.

Blessed is the one who reads the words of this prophecy, and blessed are those who hear it and take to heart what is written in it, because the time is near. (Revelation 1:3)

- **Study God's Word**

Studying the Scriptures leads to personal discoveries of God's truths. Writing down these discoveries helps one to organize and remember them.

Now the Bereans were of more noble character than the Thessalonians, for they received the message with great eagerness and examined the Scriptures every day to see if what Paul said was true. (Acts 17:11)

- **Memorize God's Word**

Memorizing God's Word enables use of the Scriptures to overcome Satan and temptations . . . to have it readily available for witnessing or helping others with a "word in season."

How can a young man keep his way pure? By living according to your word . . . I have hidden your word in my heart that I might not sin against you. (Psalm 119:9, 11)

- **Meditate on God's Word**

Meditation is used in conjunction with each of the other methods. Only as one meditates on God's Word—thinking of its meaning and application—will one discover its transforming power at work within.

> *But his delight is in the law of the LORD, and on his law he meditates day and night. He is like a tree planted by streams of water, which yields its fruit in season and whose leaf does not wither. Whatever he does prospers.* (Psalm 1:2–3)

As you explore church doctrine and examine the beliefs of the faith, always begin with the teachings and wise counsel of the source by hearing the Word, reading the Word, studying the Word, memorizing the Word, and meditating on the Word.

Maintaining Faith and Beliefs

In a recent article, Charles Colson observed that many Americans take a "salad bar" approach to Christian doctrine.[6] Much like the experience of eating at a salad bar, many Christians simply pick and choose combinations of varied doctrinal beliefs based upon their feelings of the moment, current cultural trends, or other environmental influences.

As a culture, we are often fickle and uncommitted. One partial explanation for this circumstance may be the fact that we sometimes don't actually understand what it is that we believe. We "support" certain theological positions as opposed to being fully committed to them. In an examination of "moral leadership," Robert Coles, Harvard professor of psychiatry, points to the example of Dietrich Bonhoeffer. Bonhoeffer was a German theologian who maintained his faith and his principles in the face of his impending execution by the Nazis. Coles describes the depth and essence of the faith that guided Bonhoeffer as he faced death:

> "This is the end, for me the beginning of life"—those last recorded words of Bonhoeffer's, in one of Hitler's concentration

camps, on his way to death, remind us how topsy-turvy a certain kind of moral and spiritual life can be, how utterly indifferent, even contrary, to various received secular pietism not least the psychological ones that offer us the "reality principle," and "normality" as conceptual judgments of our behavior. "Rebuked and scorned," as the biblical phrase goes, Jesus did not play it cool and cagey, did not temper His message or His behavior in order to avoid "conflict" or "anxiety" or "depression" in order to "work" on this or that "problem"; rather, He pressed on, acting on principles that to others seemed incomprehensible or dangerous, even life-threatening: the essential "madness" of a kind of ethical determination that won't settle for the rewards of social conformity. Similarly, while others (many who called themselves Christians, attended church regularly) cannily cut their views and actions to suit the political power of the day, Bonhoeffer realized that, in the words of poet Paul Celan, "death is a master from Germany"—hence the requirement of standing up to it, even if to do so defiled all that others deemed to be practical or a matter of common sense. No wonder a young Jesuit who teaches in my undergraduate course recently wished, wistfully, that the Catholic Church would one day make Dietrich Bonhoeffer its "first ecumenical saint"—a Lutheran theologian who lived as if Jesus were a concrete, nearby presence, constantly insisting that deeds, not clever-spoken or written words, not practiced rituals, are the test of a particular faith's significance in one's life.[7]

> You never know how much you really believe anything until its truth or falsehood becomes a matter of life or death. It is easy to say you believe a rope to be strong as long as you are merely using it to cord a box. But suppose you had to hang by that rope over a precipice. Wouldn't you then first discover how much you really trusted it?
>
> C. S. Lewis
> *A Grief Observed*[6]

As readers of this text, you will face varying degrees of challenge for your faith in Jesus Christ. For some that may, indeed, mean a matter of life or death. Consider, for example, the life of Cassie Bernall. This seventeen-year-old student at Columbine High School in Littleton, Colorado, was shot and killed in response to her affirmation that she believed in God. For most others, however, the challenge will come in the form of everyday decisions and interactions with friends, relatives, neighbors, loved ones, and coworkers. In the book, *True for You But Not for Me,* Paul Copan identifies some examples of inquiries and challenges that nonbelievers may pose during conversations and interaction. As Christians we need to be prepared to give an answer and to "speak the truth in love." Consider these questions and challenges:

- Who are you to judge others?
- What right do you have to convert others to your beliefs?
- Jesus is just like any other great religious leader.
- You have the right to choose your own values.
- It doesn't matter what you believe—as long as you are sincere.
- We act morally because of biological evolution or social conditioning.
- Jesus' followers fabricated the stories and sayings of Jesus.[9]

How would you respond? What do you believe? Are you prepared to give an answer?

Let the Hearer Beware

Timothy, guard what has been entrusted to your care. Turn away from godless chatter and the opposing ideas of what is falsely called knowledge, which some have professed and in so doing have wandered from the faith. Grace be with you.
(1 Timothy 6:20–21)

In the passage cited above, you see a warning for an even more sinister twist of knowledge—one that tempts you away with its clever pathways to a slightly different road to salvation. Throughout history, brilliant men and women have surfaced, even during the days immediately following Christ's time on earth, declaring many alternatives to the gospel covered by a veneer of truth. As Paul observed:

For the time will come when men will not put up with sound doctrine. Instead, to suit their own desires, they will gather around them a great number of teachers to say what their itching ears want to hear. (2 Timothy 4:3)

People are always searching for an answer, a solution, or a quick fix that will accommodate their lifestyle choices and resolve any inner conflicts about the appropriateness or correctness of their behaviors. Both in antiquity and today, people are willing to follow and pay anyone who will scratch their itching ears and tell them what they want or need to hear. In our culture, these promises and words of comfort come in the form of infomercials, bizarre religious seminars, purported communications with those who have died, and promises of prosperity, success, and happiness—you get the picture.

Credibility and Truth

If you point these things out to the brothers, you will be a good minister of Christ Jesus, brought up in the truths of the faith and of the good teaching that you have followed. (1 Timothy 4:6)

Note that the writer, Paul, is putting the responsibility squarely on the shoulders of the pastor or teacher. It is not enough for these individuals simply to tell some amusing stories with a couple of creative points or to be interesting or entertaining. Anyone communicating the gospel message should have substance and credibility, a requirement for "good teaching." Have you ever been entertained by a creative and engaging speaker, and then later realized that the speaker really had nothing important to share? This is not a new phenomenon, as Paul writes to his friend and colleague, Timothy:

Have nothing to do with godless myths and old wives' tales; rather, train yourself to be godly. (1 Timothy 4:7)

Here is an important point, particularly for those of you who may be beginning your college career. You will undoubtedly read a variety of literary works that are referred to as "classics." These are provocative pieces of literature that, for the most part, you should read. However, the challenge for all students, Christian and non-Christian, is to discern truth from such a wide assortment of creative geniuses. In many cases you will find that the greater the mind, the greater the possibility for error (embedded in skillful communication and deceptively attractive falsehoods). Consider, for example, the *Communist Manifesto* written by Karl Marx. This is a gripping text filled with many sensible quips and a tantalizing philosophy—but it is also based on many grave errors and philosophical maxims that ultimately contributed to the deaths of countless millions of people. A need for "materialism" underlies the goals of the communist philosophy and movement as communicated by Marx in the *Communist Manifesto*. This focus produced a skewed and imbalanced view on the value of the individual and societal chaos. At the same time, this book responded to the needs of the reader who desperately wanted a means of escape from his or her current living conditions. The promises of the *Communist Manifesto* scratched the ears of its readers.

Other examples of classics that you may find either fascinating or ludicrous, such as *Candide* (by Voltaire) or *Emile* (by Jean Jacques Rousseau), are fundamentally flawed. Each of these texts promotes the philosophy that human beings are "inherently good." While you may think these and other works of literature are brilliant, at their core they are flawed. By understanding these limitations and caveats, you can still glean useful information and insights from these works. They can serve as important sounding boards for your own beliefs and provide important reference points for an educated and informed community.

Christians know that the ultimate truth comes from the Bible. The challenge becomes one of sorting through the information that bombards us every day to discern what is truth and what is not.

- Truth is true—even if no one knows it.
- Truth is true—even if no one admits it.
- Truth is true—even if no one agrees as to what it is.
- Truth is true—even if no one follows it.
- Truth is true—even if no one but God grasps it fully.

The Creeds of Christianity

By definition, a creed is a brief, formal summary of the Christian faith (*Oxford English Dictionary.* 2nd ed. 20 vols. Oxford: Oxford University Press, 1989). This summary is based directly on Scripture. In the earliest stage of Christianity, creeds were also used as a criterion by which error could be exposed. Today, we can use the Christian creed as a quick reference, both as a summary and as a defense against *cults* and false religions such as Mormonism, Jehovah's Witnesses, and the New Age movement.

Starting with the key Christian doctrines, such as 1 Corinthians 8, the Christians developed creeds that would evolve into the Nicene Creed, ca. AD 325. Note the progression of the creed in the following citations of Scripture, the Apostles' Creed, and the Nicene Creed.

A Sample of Scriptures, First Century AD

The following are samplings of Scripture from the first century. As you read through these verses, make connections between this content and teaching and later statements found in the Apostles' Creed and the Nicene Creed.

Yet for us there is but one God, the Father, from whom all things came and for whom we live; and there is but one Lord, Jesus Christ, through whom all things came and through whom we live. (1 Corinthians 8:6)

Your attitude should be the same as that of Christ Jesus: Who, being in very nature God, did not consider equality with God something to be grasped, but made himself nothing, taking the very nature of a servant, being made in human likeness. And being found in appearance as a man, he humbled himself and became obedient to death—even death on a cross! Therefore God exalted him to the highest place and gave him the name that is above every name, that at the name of Jesus every knee should bow, in heaven and on earth and under the earth, and every tongue confess that Jesus Christ is Lord, to the glory of God the Father. (Philippians 2:5–11)

For there is one God and one mediator between God and men, the man Christ Jesus, who gave himself as a ransom for all men—the testimony given in its proper time. (1 Timothy 2:5–6)

Beyond all question, the mystery of godliness is great: He appeared in a body, was vindicated by the Spirit, was seen by angels, was preached among the nations, was believed on in the world, was taken up in glory. (1 Timothy 3:16)

The Apostles' Creed

The Apostles' Creed was an expansion of ancient baptismal questions first used in the church at Rome:

I believe in God, the Father Almighty, the Creator of heaven and earth, and in Jesus Christ his only Son, our Lord: Who was conceived by the Holy Spirit, born of the Virgin Mary, suffered under Pontius Pilate, was crucified, died, and was buried. He descended into hell; the third day he rose again from the dead; he ascended into heaven and sits at the right hand of God the Father Almighty, from there he shall come to judge the living and the dead. I believe in the Holy Spirit, the holy catholic church, the communion of saints, the forgiveness of sins, the resurrection of the body, and life everlasting. Amen.

The Nicene Creed

The Nicene Creed was named after a council of church leaders which met at Nicæa in AD 325. The Council of Chalcedon officially endorsed an expanded form of this creed in AD 451. Both cities are in northern Turkey, just east of Istanbul (ancient Constantinople, the Christian center built by the first Christian Roman emperor, Constantine, ca. 330). Constantine called the Council of Nicæa to put an end to squabbles among church leaders over the nature of Christ. He wanted answers based firmly on the Bible, not traditions or fancy interpretations (which had become heresies).

We believe in one God, the Father Almighty, maker of heaven and earth, of all that is seen and unseen. We believe in one Lord Jesus Christ, the only begotten Son of God, begotten of His Father before all worlds, God of God, Light of Light, very God of very God, begotten, not made, being of one substance with the Father, by whom all things were made; who for us men and for our salvation, came down from heaven, and was incarnate by the Holy Spirit of the Virgin Mary, and was made man. For our sake he was crucified under Pontius Pilate. He suffered and was buried. On the third day he rose again in accordance with the Scriptures; he ascended into heaven and is seated at the right hand of the Father. He will come again, with glory, to judge the living and the dead; whose kingdom shall have no end. We believe in the Holy Spirit, the Lord, and the Giver of Life, who proceeds from the Father and the Son. With the Father and the Son he is worshipped and glorified. He has spoken through the Prophets. We believe in one holy catholic and apostolic Church. We acknowledge one baptism for the forgiveness of sins. We look for the resurrection of the dead, and the life of the world to come. Amen.

A Connection Worth Noting

These creeds are not the original source for Christian doctrines but rather reflect an accurate summary. They were outlines endorsed by the early church leaders, and are still consulted by many branches of Christianity today. These creeds serve as the sources for contemporary "statements of faith" adopted by most Protestant denominations and Christian organizations. As you study the New

Testament, mark those passages that serve as a direct foundation for the creeds of Christianity.

On Standing

As a six-year-old sitting in a little country church, I absorbed a skeletal framework of the Apostles' Creed—not enough to claim that I actually knew it, but enough to get through a few lines with the adults who spoke it in staccato rhythm from their pews each Sunday morning: *"I believe in God the Father . . . Creation of heaven and earth . . . His only Son . . . crucified, dead, and buried. He descended into hell . . . He ascended into heaven . . . life everlasting."* I've never gotten around to memorizing the whole creed, partly because I'm lazy and partly because I tend to abhor the practices of preceding generations. Even so, when I really sit down and think about it, I get the sense that those ancients in my country church had something right.

People today have mantras and credos, but Christians in general have strayed away from this custom of creeds. Sometime between the poodle skirt era and the digital age, it became politically incorrect to stand in a congregation and say, "I believe." Believing has become discriminatory, and having faith that one way is the only way has become unacceptable. Under the critical eye of more tolerant religions, the identity Christians once found in a collective and concrete faith has been bruised. We doubt the legitimacy of our faith in comparison to others. We speak of Christ as we would a fable or a fairy tale.

Perhaps it's time for us to get back to this idea of creeds—not as ammunition against the religion down the street, but as tonic to get our blood circulating again. It is always helpful to hear the person on our left affirming our faith. Sometimes it is vital. Some days, there's nothing better than a measured beat from the person at our back. It reminds us of what we believe and why we believe it. It gives us the courage to stand and say again, "I believe."

—Lisa Velthouse

FAQ

Q. Where can I find a simple list of the essential doctrines of Christianity?

A. The best summary is perhaps the Nicene Creed, sometimes mistakenly called the Apostles' Creed. Many churches and denominations recite the Nicene Creed during their worship services or have it printed in their hymnals. The authors of this creed were church leaders from the fourth century AD. They drafted it to reflect the substance of 1 Corinthians 8 and related passages.

Q. If the vast majority of Christians have embraced the same list of basic truths, then why are there so many "brands" of Christians?

A. These "brands" of Christians are referred to as denominations. For example, Baptists, Episcopalians, Presbyterians, Wesleyans, Methodists, and Nazarenes are but a few of these denominations. These groups or "Christian sects" may differ over interpretations of certain passages which in turn give them unique doctrines. They may place a stronger emphasis on a certain aspect of Christ's instructions than do other groups, but they still endorse the foundational truths of the Nicene Creed.

This is similar to American politics. Republicans and Democrats and other "officially" organized political parties have their differences, but still endorse the Constitution as the basic standard for the United States' political framework. Although these various interpretations of the Constitution may offer divergent views on the nature of States' rights, they all heartily endorse and embrace the notion of popular elections, the presidency, a representative Congress, and a system of governmental checks and balances. Because they endorse these fundamentals and others, they are easily associated with democracy.

In the same light, we can easily identify various denominations within Christianity. One denomination may place more emphasis on rituals and the sacraments, another group may stress sharing the gospel through personal encounters with non-Christians, and yet another may focus on the care of poor people; yet they all hold as a central truth the reality of the Trinity and a belief in Jesus Christ's Resurrection.

Q. Is Catholicism a denomination?

A. No. Most people associate "denomination" with Protestantism, a movement of Christianity that developed in Europe during the sixteenth century. Prior to that period, known by historians as the Reformation, there were two great branches of Christianity. The oldest of these branches is Eastern Orthodoxy, which claims to have originated shortly after the time of Christ. Over the centuries the Orthodox tradition has sub-divided into several ethnic or national groups. There are Greek, Russian, Syrian, and Coptic (Egyptian) Orthodox churches still in existence today. These Christians place heavy emphasis on rituals and cultural identity as the marks of a true Christian.

A second branch of Christianity developed when Christians in Western Europe claimed that the bishop of Rome was the earthly head of the Church. They made their case from the early tradition that St. Peter had lived and died in Rome and that Rome was the capital city of the Empire. Eventually they split from the Orthodox Church and became Roman Catholics. Their understanding of salvation centers on a cooperative effort between God and humans. While the good merit of Jesus Christ's death is necessary for salvation, it is not enough. Human beings must also contribute their own merits of repentance and good works in order to attain eternal life.

"Protestants," initially led by Martin Luther, a Catholic priest, called upon the church leaders, namely the pope, to reform the Church's doctrines in closer conformity to those found in the New Testament itself. You might say that Luther was asking them to "consider the source."

When Luther's followers and the powerful Roman Catholic Church (with its headquarters at the Vatican in Rome, Italy) could not settle their differences, those in protest (the Protestants) either left the Roman Catholic Church or the pope excommunicated them. What resulted are three great branches of Christianity, with the third—Protestantism—divided into many denominations.

Q. Will Christians who are not Protestants be in heaven?

A. Of course! God has set forth certain standards and a clear plan of salvation in His Word, the Bible. The destination of each person's soul will be judged by these same standards, and not by one's affiliation with any earthly church. Whether a person is Russian Orthodox, Roman Catholic, or a member of a Protestant denomination is not the criteria for eternal life given by God through the New Testament authors. Rather, God looks at each person's heart. Only God knows who will enter heaven. The same source to which Christians have appealed for 2,000 years is available to you:

For the word of God is living and active. Sharper than any double-edged sword, it penetrates even to dividing soul and spirit, joints and marrow; it judges the thoughts and attitudes of the heart. Nothing in all creation is hidden from God's sight. Everything is uncovered and laid bare before the eyes of him to whom we must give account. (Hebrews 4:12–13)

Blessed are the pure in heart, for they will see God. (Matthew 5:8)

For where your treasure is, there your heart will be also. (Matthew 6:21)

Then they prayed, "Lord, you know everyone's heart. Show us which of these two you have chosen." (Acts 1:24)

God, who knows the heart, showed that he accepted them by giving the Holy Spirit to them, just as he did to us. (Acts 15:8)

Q. How can Christians who all claim to follow Christ have such different views of salvation?

A. All Christians believe that salvation comes by faith. But faith can be understood in different ways. Orthodox Christians see faith as primarily a birthright from being born into a family and community of believers and then adhering to the doctrines and rituals of that tradition. Roman Catholics understand faith to be a human response to God's love. Salvation comes through participation in the sacraments, primarily baptism and Holy Communion, as well as good works done as a demonstration of one's faithfulness to God.

Luther and the Protestants who came after him argued that salvation was a matter of faith in what God has done for us apart from any works on our part. It was trust in God's forgiving work on the cross that saved us; nothing else was necessary. Luther believed the Bible teaches that a person is established as just—acquitted of the guilt of sins—by placing faith in Jesus Christ, His life, death, and Resurrection. While studying the writings of the Apostle Paul in the New Testament, Luther discovered an error in the Roman Catholic's stated doctrine of justification. As you read through the following passages, note the clear picture of salvation by faith:

But now a righteousness from God, apart from law, has been made known, to which the Law and the Prophets testify. This righteousness from God comes through faith in Jesus Christ to all who believe. There is no difference, for all have sinned and fall short of the glory of God, and are justified freely by his grace through the redemption that came by Christ Jesus. God presented him as a sacrifice of atonement, through faith in his blood. (Romans 3:21–25a)

Therefore, since we have been justified through faith, we have peace with God through our Lord Jesus Christ, through whom we have gained access by faith into this grace in which we now stand. (Romans 5:1–2a)

"The word is near you; it is in your mouth and in your heart," that is, the word of faith we are proclaiming: That if you confess with your mouth, "Jesus is Lord," and believe in your heart that God raised him from the dead, you will be saved. For it is with your heart that you believe and are justified, and it is with your mouth that you confess and are saved. (Romans 10:8–10)

But because of his great love for us, God, who is rich in mercy, made us alive with Christ even when we were dead in transgressions . . . it is by grace you have been saved, through faith—and this not from yourselves, it is the gift of God—not by works, so that no one can boast. (Ephesians 2:4–5, 8–9)

Q. What should our attitude be toward Christians who differ from us in their view of salvation?

A. We must first determine whether they hold to the basic truths of Christianity as expressed in "the source"—the Bible—and as summarized in the great creeds of Christianity. There are those who claim to be followers of Christ who deny His divinity, His Resurrection and His power to save us from sin. Other so-called Christians belong to cults that reject biblical teaching for their own doctrines (see below).

For those Christians who share a common creed, we must show love, respect, and a sincere desire to discover the best interpretation of the teachings of the Bible. There are Orthodox and Catholics who do trust in Christ for salvation. There are Protestants who have drifted away from biblical teaching and believe that salvation comes by belonging to a denomination or doing good works. Together we should "consider the source" and come to a clearer understanding of what the Bible teaches.

Official dialogue between Catholics and Protestants about the meaning of salvation has been taking place in recent years. By identifying overreactions in both branches of Christianity and by genuinely seeking common ground, bridges of understanding are now being built. For an evangelical Catholic's perspective, you might consult Keith Fournier's "Evangelical Catholic: A Contradiction in Terms?" (in *Evangelical Catholics*, pp. 11–23).

In May 1999, the Catholics signed the Catholic-Lutheran Accord, which represents a major step in resolving the difference between Protestants and Catholics on how one is made righteous in the sight of God. Numerous Web sites discuss this important yet complicated issue.

Your Catholic friends who are active in their church and parish most likely have made a faith commitment to Christ in the same manner as Protestant Christians. They have placed their faith in the Christ of history and believe in His Resurrection and atoning blood—the power to save our sins and give us eternal life. Their faith may be as vibrant as that of the disciples and their lives as devoted to Christ as Mother Teresa's. While the official doctrines between the Roman Catholic Church, and, say, the Baptists, are at odds, the daily beliefs may not be that far apart. A good example is Promise Keepers—the men's movement that has been joined by millions, Catholic and

Protestant alike. These men endorse the fundamental tenets of Christianity, such as those you'll find in the creeds described above and outlined in modern books like Chuck Colson's *Being the Body* (W Publishing Group/Thomas Nelson, 2003).

Q. What is the difference between a *denomination* and a *cult*?

A. As we have explained above, denominations differ on their interpretation of various scriptural passages, but they would all agree to the basic tenets of Christianity as outlined in the creeds. Cults are religious groups whose founders have rejected one or more of the central teachings of Christianity. For example, Jehovah's Witnesses do not accept the fact that Jesus Christ is the second person of the Trinity, co-equal with the Father. Instead, they hold that while Jesus was divine, He was a lesser god, created in time and, therefore, not eternal. Christian Scientists deny the reality of evil and an Evil One, Satan. The cults often adopt much of Christian teaching and ethics; however, we cannot accept them as members of the Christian faith because they have rejected one or more of the orthodox teachings of Christianity.

Reaction and Reflection

It is valuable and useful to set aside time in our lives for the purpose of examining our faith and our beliefs. In this portion of our Reaction and Reflection (R & R) experience, we encourage you to think about your faith, where it came from, and where you are taking your faith as a believer in Jesus Christ. As always, if these questions provide the need for additional counsel and discussion, we encourage you to make contact with a friend, relative, pastor, or teacher for that assistance.

1. What are the roots of your Christian faith (i.e., who are the people or organizations that have been crucial to your learning about God)?

2. Obtain a copy of the doctrinal beliefs for your local church (or denomination). If this is not readily available, copies often can be obtained through Internet web pages. What does your church/denomination believe about the following areas of doctrine?

God

Jesus Christ

the Holy Spirit

salvation

man

creation

the Bible

sin

Satan

church

3. Sit down with a friend and discuss the similarities and differences that may exist between your denominational beliefs. What did you learn?

Suggested Readings and Resources

Books

Alexander, D., and P. Alexander, eds. *Zondervan Handbook to the Bible*. Grand Rapids, MI: Zondervan, 1999.

Broderick, R. C., and V. Broderick, eds. *The Catholic Encyclopedia*. New York: Thomas Nelson, 1990.

Bruce, F. F. *The Books and the Parchments: How We Got Our English Bible*. Grand Rapids, MI: Revell, 1984.

Colson, C., and E. Vaughn. *Being the Body*. Grand Rapids, MI: W Publishing Group/Thomas Nelson, 2003.

Craigie, P. C. *The Old Testament: Its Background, Growth, and Content*. Nashville: Abingdon Press, 2000.

Drane, J. *Introducing the New Testament*. Minneapolis, MN: Augsburg Fortress Press, 2001.

———. *Introducing the Old Testament*. Minneapolis, MN: Augsburg Fortress Press, 2002.

Earle, R. H. *How We Got Our Bible*. Kansas City, MO: Beacon Hill Press, 1997.

Fournier, K., and C. Colson. *Evangelical Catholics*. Nashville: Thomas Nelson, 1990.

Geisler, N. L., and W. E. Nix. *A General Introduction to the Bible*. Chicago: Moody Publishers, 1968.

Gundry, R. H. *A Survey of the New Testament*. 3rd ed. Grand Rapids, MI: Zondervan, 1994.

Hamilton, V. P. *Handbook on the Pentateuch*. Grand Rapids, MI: Baker Book House, 1982.

Kelly, J. N. D. *Early Christian Creeds*. 3rd ed. Boston: Addison-Wesley, 1989.

Kennedy, J. D. *Why I Believe*. Nashville: Word Publishing, 1999.

Lewis, C. S. *Mere Christianity*. San Francisco: Harper, 2001. First published 1943 by MacMillan.

Little, P. *Know What You Believe*. Rev. ed. Downers Grove, IL: InterVarsity, 2000.

McDowell, J. *The New Evidence That Demands a Verdict*. Nashville: Nelson Reference, 1999.

Metzger, B. M. *The Text of the New Testament: Its Transmission, Corruption, and Restoration*. New York: Oxford University Press, 1992.

Schaeffer, F. A. *The Complete Works of Francis A. Schaeffer: A Christian Worldview*. Wheaton, IL: Crossway Books, 1982.

Schultz, S. J. *The Old Testament Speaks*. 5th ed. New York: Harper Collins, 1999.

Stott, J. R. W. *Basic Christianity*. Rev. ed. Grand Rapids, MI: Wm. B. Eerdmans Publisher, 1986.

Tenney, M. C., and W. M. Dunnett. *New Testament Survey*. Rev. ed. Grand Rapids, MI: Wm. B. Eerdmans Publisher, 1985.

Wilkins, M. J., and J. P. Moreland, eds. *Jesus Under Fire*. Grand Rapids, MI: Zondervan, 1996.

Yamauchi, E. *Harper's World of the New Testament*. New York: Harper Collins, 1981.

Other Resources

Bible Gateway. http://www.biblegateway.com (accessed August 5, 2007).

Books and Culture: A Christian Review. Magazine published bimonthly. Also available online at http://www.christianity.com/books (accessed August 5, 2007).

Christianity Today. Magazine published monthly. Also available online at http://www.christianitytoday.com/ct (accessed August 5, 2007)

Christian History & Biography. Magazine published quarterly. Also available online at http://www.christianitytoday.com/history (accessed August 5, 2007).

Endnotes—note form

1. The Barna Group. http://www.barna.org (accessed August 5, 2007).

2. The Barna Group. http://www.barna.org (accessed August 5, 2007).

3. Renovaré. http://www.renovare.org/journey_spiritual_formation_ groups_disciplines.htm (accessed August 5, 2007).

4. Grant R. Osborne, *The Hermeneutical Spiral: A Comprehensive Introduction to Biblical Interpretation* (Downers Grove, IL: InterVarsity Press, 1991), 6.

5. "The Word Hand" was developed by The Navigators. Information regarding this approach (and the descriptions cited) to understanding God's Word can be found at http://www.navigators.org/us/resources (accessed August 5, 2007).

6. Charles Colson, "Salad-Bar Christianity," *Christianity Today*, August 7, 2000, in the Wilberforce Forum.

7. Robert Coles, *Lives of Moral Leadership: Lives of Men and Women Who Have Made a Difference* (New York: Random House, 2000), 200.

8. C. S. Lewis, *A Grief Observed* (San Francisco: Harper, 1994), reprint ed. 22-23.

9. Paul Copan, chapter titles, in *True for You But Not for Me: Deflating the Slogans That Leave Christians Speechless* (Minneapolis: Bethany House Publishers, 1998).

understanding the basics

salvation

*I tell you the truth, no one can see the kingdom
of God unless he is born again.*
(John 3:3)

a daytona beach memory:
stumbling over an opportunity

Stumbling over a couple at night on Daytona Beach seemed to present a great opportunity to "evangelize." I pulled out my worn *Four Spiritual Laws* booklet and flashlight. It was Spring Break 1978, and thousands of collegians were there to party. Another group, considerably smaller, was there to tell the partiers about "the plan of salvation."

As a zealous new Christian, I proudly asked the embarrassed girl peeking from beneath a sand-encrusted blanket—"If you died today, would you go to heaven or hell?" She sheepishly replied, "Uh, I'm not sure, and, um . . ." Her blanketed new "friend" piped in, "*&%#**.#@%^**!!" My response was defensive. "I was hoping to tell you the good news," I said.

She was visibly upset with her surly associate and asked him to stop and listen. "Okay," he snapped. "Tell us the *g-oo-oo-ood newwws*. And make it the short version." I was naïve and not the most articulate evangelist, but I met his challenge. "The Bible says if you're living in sin, you're going to hell." Before I could continue, he yelled, "Of all the *&#*^@** nerve!"

I took my flashlight and began to leave, for my own survival more than anything else. Then she called out, perhaps in guilt, maybe in curiosity . . . but she called. "Wait! Please tell me what you were going to say."

It was an awkward situation—a dark and unforgettable spring break night. Two college students barely acquainted making out in a public place. A third collegian—me—stumbling into the situation after praying for a chance to "witness." Only two of us wanted to talk about religion. The third, a strapping puka-shelled mook, cursed the very name of God.

Excusing myself while they made themselves presentable, I ran back to my nearby hotel room and grabbed some pop and munchies, a second flashlight, and another booklet.

The couple sat and munched with me, eventually laughing about the turn of events. As the already late night wore on, I continued through the booklet. She became serious about the "salvation plan" and becoming a Christian. He began to lose interest and excused himself. She commented that for the first time she understood what it meant to be "saved," to accept salvation. Following the booklet's guidelines, we prayed together and she became a Christian.

She shared that the only reason she was underneath the blanket was to feel accepted, in a sense, to meet the personal need of belonging. The last time I saw her, she was carrying her blanket and sandals, alone, with a curled brown booklet also in her grasp. She had found answers she had longed for, the clearly defined essentials of salvation.

This chapter helps to explain this same plan, along with a fuller understanding of the doctrine of salvation.

On the last night of that spring break, a collegian overdosed and jumped from a hotel roof to his death, a few feet from the pool. Leaving that sad scene, I couldn't help but think of the beach discussion a couple nights earlier, and the guy's rejection of the plan of salvation. "If he had been that student dead by the pool, would he have missed not only the pool, but heaven?"

A honking, swerving car cruised by with shirtless beach boys hanging out the windows, yelling crude pickup lines. I locked eyes with one of riders, the same fellow who had cursed me from the beach blanket. He launched a tirade of slurred curse words at me and kept shouting and flipping me off as they pulled away.

That was the last time I saw him. Preferring temporary pleasures over inner peace and lasting joy, he had rejected the plan of salvation. The good part about this story is that it took place 25 years ago. Perhaps he has returned to those questions we discussed on that bizarre night. The plan of salvation doesn't change. We do.

understanding the basics

salvation

 Consider the Source

I tell you the truth, no one can see the kingdom of God unless he is born again. (John 3:3)

Therefore, if anyone is in Christ, he is a new creation; the old has gone, the new has come! (2 Corinthians 5:17)

Perhaps you are familiar with the term "born again." In most Protestant circles it carries the same meaning as the descriptions provided in the verses above. God's Word tells us that anyone can become a brand-new person—a Christian, a believer in Jesus Christ.

 Understand the Need

One of the most basic and critical doctrines of Christianity is salvation. The beliefs and principles of Christianity pivot on several key areas, including our understandings of God the Father and Jesus His Son, the crucifixion of Jesus on our behalf for the forgiveness of sin, the Resurrection, God's love and grace, our regeneration when we are "born again" through salvation, and the promise of forgiveness and eternal life. All of these important areas connect directly with the doctrine of salvation.

There is a tendency for us to assume that Christians have a common set of beliefs and expectations about salvation. When surveyed about their own salvation and the reasons why people "go to heaven," individuals who identified themselves as having a personal relationship with Jesus gave the following responses: 61% said they would go to heaven because Jesus is their personal Savior, 10% felt they would go to heaven because they are basically good, 12% expressed some uncertainty as to what would happen to them when they died, 6% felt that God would allow everyone into heaven even in the absence of a salvation experience, 5% believed they would go to heaven because they tried to obey the Ten Commandments, 2% did not believe they would go to heaven, and others were unsure.[1] Do you find these results surprising in any way?

Once again, we must return to the source of truth: God's Word. As we proceed through this examination of salvation, take the time to consider and clarify your beliefs. We begin this discussion by clarifying the nature of man in relation to sin and to God:

For all have sinned and fall short of the glory of God. (Romans 3:23)

We all, like sheep, have gone astray, each of us has turned to his own way . . . (Isaiah 53:6)

Jesus shared the command to be born again (John 3:3) because we all have been separated from God by sin. This was not God's original design for us. But because of a sinful act by Adam and Eve (the first two humans according to biblical accounts), mankind's normal relationship with God changed, a relationship He had designed. This normal relationship between God and the first man and woman is referred to as "the creation account," and is recorded in the Old Testament book of Genesis. When Adam and Eve sinned, "willfully disobeying God," humanity's close relationship with God was broken. Even today, everyone is born with a moral flaw in his or her very nature. We have a void where God once was—instead of a natural desire to love and serve God, we are naturally inclined to sin and to disobey God's commands. Jesus died, having never sinned, to help us once again bridge this gap between ourselves and God:

> *But God demonstrates His own love for us in this: While we were still sinners, Christ died for us.* (Romans 5:8)

> *I am the way and the truth and the life. No one comes to the Father except through me.* (John 14:6)

The starting point to establishing a relationship with God is to acknowledge that we too have "gone astray" (Isaiah 53:6) and have sinned against God. But it is not enough for us simply to acknowledge that we are sinners. Even the wickedest people are often willing to acknowledge that they are doing wrong. True repentance requires that we also admit we are helpless to save ourselves. The way to forgiveness opens to us when we stop trying to be righteous through our own efforts. Instead, we come to believe that God loved us as sinners and provided the only means for us to be in a relationship with Him through Jesus—"the way" (John 14:6).

Christ's Words on Salvation

Jesus Christ made it very clear that He was the Messiah. His proclamation was not just for His peers, but for all generations. And according to Christ's own recorded statements, accepting Him into our hearts is the ONLY way to enter heaven. Consider the dialogue between Jesus and Nicodemus:

> *Now there was a man of the Pharisees named Nicodemus, a member of the Jewish ruling council. He came to Jesus at night and said, "Rabbi, we know you are a teacher who has come from God. For no one could perform the miraculous signs you are doing if God were not with him."*

> *In reply Jesus declared, "I tell you the truth, no one can see the kingdom of God unless he is born again."*

"How can a man be born when he is old?" Nicodemus
asked. *"Surely he cannot enter a second time into his
mother's womb to be born!"*

Jesus answered, *"I tell you the truth, no one can enter the
kingdom of God unless he is born of water and the Spirit.
Flesh gives birth to flesh, but the Spirit gives birth to spirit.
You should not be surprised at my saying, 'You must be born
again.' The wind blows wherever it pleases. You hear its
sound, but you cannot tell where it comes from or where it is
going. So it is with everyone born of the Spirit."*

"How can this be?" Nicodemus asked.

"You are Israel's teacher," said Jesus, *"and do you not
understand these things? I tell you the truth, we speak of what
we know, and we testify to what we have seen, but still you
people do not accept our testimony. I have spoken to you of
earthly things and you do not believe; how then will you
believe if I speak of heavenly things? No one has ever gone
into heaven except the one who came from heaven—the Son of
Man. Just as Moses lifted up the snake in the desert, so the Son
of Man must be lifted up, that everyone who believes in him
may have eternal life. For God so loved the world that he gave
his one and only Son, that whoever believes in him shall not
perish but have eternal life. For God did not send his Son into
the world to condemn the world, but to save the world through
him. Whoever believes in him is not condemned, but whoever
does not believe stands condemned already because he has not
believed in the name of God's one and only Son. This is the
verdict: Light has come into the world, but men loved darkness
instead of light because their deeds were evil. Everyone who
does evil hates the light, and will not come into the light for
fear that his deeds will be exposed. But whoever lives by the
truth comes into the light, so that it may be seen plainly that
what he has done has been done through God."* (John 3:1–21)

After reading the story of Nicodemus, and the previous verses, what questions do you have? Perhaps the next section will help you find answers. The New Testament Scriptures are clear in identifying the actions required to become a Christian:

In the past God overlooked such ignorance, but now he commands all people everywhere to repent. (Acts 17:30)

Whoever believes in the Son [Jesus Christ, the Son of God] has eternal life, but whoever rejects the Son will not see life, for God's wrath remains on him. (John 3:36)

That if you confess with your mouth, "Jesus is Lord," and believe in your heart that God raised him from the dead, you will be saved. (Romans 10:9)

Yet to all who received him, to those who believed in his name, he gave the right to become children of God. (John 1:12)

Bill Bright and Campus Crusade International created a simple and easily understandable model for sharing the good news of salvation. The "Four Spiritual Laws" provide a way of getting to the most basic understanding of salvation and what we need to do to establish a personal relationship with Jesus Christ:

The Four Spiritual Laws

- **Law #1:** God loves you, and offers a wonderful plan for your life. (John 3:16; John 10:10)
- **Law #2:** Man is sinful and separated from God. Therefore, he cannot know and experience God's love and plan for his life. (Romans 3:23; Romans 6:23)
- **Law #3:** Jesus Christ is God's only provision for man's sin. Through Him you can know and experience God's love and plan for your life. (Romans 5:8; 1 Corinthians 15:3–6; John 14:6)

- **Law #4:** We must individually receive Jesus Christ as Savior and Lord; then we can know and experience God's love and plan for our lives. (John 1:12; Ephesians 2:8–9; John 3:1–8; Revelation 3:20)[2]

Personally Receiving Christ

If you have already asked Christ into your life, you are assured of eternal life as He has promised:

Do not let your hearts be troubled. Trust in God; trust also in me. In my Father's house are many rooms; if it were not so, I would have told you. I am going to prepare a place for you. And if I go and prepare a place for you, I will come back and take you to be with me that you may also be where I am. You know the way to the place where I am going. (John 14:1–4)

If you have accepted Christ, you are assured of His presence in your heart.

We know that we live in him and he in us, because he has given us of his Spirit. And we have seen and testify that the Father has sent his Son to be the Savior of the world. If anyone acknowledges that Jesus is the Son of God, God lives in him and he in God. And so we know and rely on the love God has for us . . . (1 John 4:13–16)

For God so loved the world that he gave his one and only Son, that whoever believes in him shall not perish but have eternal life. (John 3:16)

The latter passage is rather direct, clarifying the *doctrine* of *salvation*, and it is perhaps the most quoted verse of the Bible. Simply put, if you ask Christ to come into your life, you will go to heaven. If you do not, you will go to hell. But Christ's promises also apply to man's immediate situation: a more fulfilling life while here on earth and a way to find contentment.

I have come that they may have life, and have it to the full.
(John 10:10b)

Keep your lives free from the love of money and be content with what you have, because God has said, "Never will I leave you; never will I forsake you." (Hebrews 13:5)

Consider two New Testament accounts of persons who accepted Christ. The first dialogue occurred during the crucifixion of Christ. The second took place while the Apostle Paul and Silas were imprisoned, a punishment for their public defense of the doctrines of Christ.

The Crucifixion Dialogue

One of the criminals who hung there hurled insults at him: "Aren't you the Christ? Save yourself and us!"

But the other criminal rebuked him. "Don't you fear God," he said, "since you are under the same sentence? We are punished justly, for we are getting what our deeds deserve. But this man has done nothing wrong."

Then he said, "Jesus, remember me when you come into your kingdom."

Jesus answered him, "I tell you the truth, today you will be with me in paradise." (Luke 23:39–43)

Paul and Silas in the Philippian Jail

The crowd joined in the attack against Paul and Silas, and the magistrates ordered them to be stripped and beaten. After they had been severely flogged, they were thrown into prison, and the jailer was commanded to guard them carefully. Upon receiving such orders, he put them in the inner cell and fastened their feet in the stocks.

About midnight Paul and Silas were praying and singing hymns to God, and the other prisoners were listening to them. Suddenly there was such a violent earthquake that the foundations of the prison were shaken. At once all the prison doors flew open, and everybody's chains came loose. The jailer woke up, and when he saw the prison doors open, he drew his sword and was about to kill himself because he thought the prisoners had escaped. But Paul shouted, "Don't harm yourself! We are all here!"

The jailer called for lights, rushed in and fell trembling before Paul and Silas. He then brought them out and asked, "Sirs, what must I do to be saved?"

They replied, "Believe in the Lord Jesus, and you will be saved—you and your household." Then they spoke the word of the Lord to him and to all the others in his house. At that hour of the night the jailer took them and washed their wounds; then immediately he and all his family were baptized. The jailer brought them into his house and set a meal before them; he was filled with joy because he had come to believe in God—he and his whole family. (Acts 16:22–34)

In the first account, one criminal insults and rejects Jesus. The second criminal defends Jesus, acknowledges his own sin and culpability, and asks Jesus to remember him. Jesus immediately responds to the penitent criminal and accepts his statement of faith.

In the second account, the jailer is brought to faith by a cataclysmic event. Trembling, he asks specifically what he must do to be saved. He realizes that Paul and Silas hold the key to a totally different way of life. When he listens and accepts "the word of the Lord to him," he and his household are immediately baptized.

We also should look at a New Testament passage that describes one person's encounter with the good news of salvation and his subsequent struggle with the implications of trusting in Christ. The book of Acts provides an overview of the early church during the years immediately following Christ's Resurrection. Paul and Peter are the key church leaders. Near the end of this book (Acts 26; see also 25:13–27), we are given an account of the Apostle Paul explaining Christ's life and teachings to different Roman leaders at Caesarea (on the coast of modern Israel). These leaders include Festus, the procurator of Judea, King Agrippa II, and Bernice, Agrippa's companion. King Agrippa responds to Paul's comments in this way:

> *"Do you think in such a short time you can persuade me to be a Christian?" Paul replied, "Short time or long—I pray God that not only you but all who are listening to me today may become what I am, except for these chains."* (Acts 26:28–29).

We can imagine a bantering tone in Agrippa's voice, perhaps a smile and an upraised eyebrow. However, it is not Agrippa who interrupts Paul's discourse, but Festus. It is interesting to note that Paul is allowed to speak freely and at length. Unlike the beach boy who cut me off before I could even launch into my message, King Agrippa listens to Paul's message. He doesn't denigrate Paul as Festus does, but expresses interest in what Paul has to say. One can only wonder what might have been going on in Agrippa's mind before Festus derailed his thoughts.

Christian reader, can you recall a time before your actual conversion when you flirted with Christianity, perhaps in the same way that King Agrippa does in the above passage? What finally made the difference in your life?

And for non-Christian readers, do you have any thoughts similar to those of Agrippa or the jailer? We encourage you to find a Christian friend and discuss any questions you might have. Perhaps your friend can lead you to other helpful Scriptures and answer some of your questions about having a personal relationship with Jesus Christ.

On Introducing

I remember those special missionary services. They were packed full of illustrations (mostly vivid word pictures) depicting sacrificial service, miraculous healings, and marvelous provisions. Some accounts were related with tearful emotion, some engaged the listener in awesome suspense, while others glowed with enthusiasm and excitement. The individual components of the service led up to a climactic point in which the leader passionately appealed to the audience — "All who want to give their lives to God for His service, please come forward." Wow, was I scared! I just knew as soon as I responded to the invitation, within reach of the altar I would hear God's voice asking me to go to Africa for the rest of my life. At the moment, it really shook me up. As a teenager, I was quite satisfied with the comforts and security of my home and country. But, in one "consecration service" after another, I released my grip on the back of the seat in front of me, walked slowly down the aisle, and kneeled beside a long line of teens whose sensitive spirits had responded as mine did.

I never actually heard a specific calling to any certain geographic region during those contemplative prayer times at the altar. And, even though the idea of going to Africa or some other far-away place overwhelmed my heart and mind, I learned some wonderful things from those experiences. I discovered that I have an awesome responsibility to respect "those who are called." Being called to full-time Christian service as a minister or missionary is a high honor to be taken seriously. Those whose major work is consumed with sharing Jesus and His love with congregations, families, and individuals have multiple opportunities to introduce. I learned what it is like to "be still" in God's presence so I can hear His words of direction and encouragement. I also discovered that I must be a committee of one to introduce others to my best friend, Jesus Christ. I am called first to be a Christian — a witness of Christ's transforming power, an example of Christ-likeness that attracts my work companions, friends, and even total strangers to catch a glimpse of the Jesus in me.

Have you seen Jesus in a pastor or similar full-time servant? Most certainly! Have you seen Jesus in a grocery clerk, office receptionist, truck driver, school teacher or another student? Absolutely! In a sense every human being is looking for Jesus. Has anyone seen Jesus in *you*?

The words of a consecration chorus I remember still ring in my ears and echo in my heart, *"Lord, lay some soul upon my heart, and touch that soul through me. And may I humbly do my part to win that soul for Thee."*

FAQ

Q. What is an easy way to understand this "fallen nature" inherent in all human beings?

A. Simple observation of the world around us reveals that human beings are naturally inclined to be self-centered and resistant to obeying the rules. This is most apparent in small children, but surfaces in adults as well (e.g., "road rage," dishonesty, "cheating" in relationships). This sinful nature, a result of "the Fall," is much like a car that is out of alignment. When we take our hands off the steering wheel, there is a natural tendency for the car to go astray. In one of his hymns, Charles Wesley describes it as "our bent to sinning." It is a well-observed fact that human beings are morally and spiritually inclined to gratify their own desires rather than submit to the will and ways of God.

Q. Do people lose their sinful nature when they become Christians?

A. Not instantaneously or completely. But the purpose of salvation, as we have discussed it, is not only to give us eternal life, but also to enable us to become more like Christ in this life. Although the inclination to disobey is within us, even as Christians, God gives us the spiritual power to overcome sin and to follow His commands. As we mature in our faith, the desire to serve Christ becomes greater and godliness becomes the pattern of our life.

Q. How can I ever learn all of the Christian teachings, let alone understand them?

A. One does not need to learn all of the Christian teachings before becoming a Christian. In fact, few Christians ever learn all of them, and some things we can only understand in part.

Now we see but a poor reflection as in a mirror; then we shall see face to face. Now I know in part; then I shall know fully, even as I am fully known. (1 Corinthians 13:12)

This passage implies that we see enough to know Christ's teachings are true. We may not know all the details, but we know enough to want to put our trust in Him. Accordingly, the above Scripture declares that in heaven Christians "shall know fully."

 ## Reaction and Reflection

If you have not put your faith in Christ, and you desire to do so, you can by praying to Him, even at this very moment. Ask Him to come into your heart and life, and to forgive you of your sins. If you become a Christian, share your decision with a Christian friend and ask a pastor, one of your professors, or a spiritual leader about discipleship—a personally guided approach to spiritual growth (discussed more fully in chapter 8 of this text). Also, begin studying the source for yourself. The book of John is a good place to start. John represents many of Christ's actions while on earth, and contains a thorough collection of teachings.

If you have been a Christian for some time, take a few moments to conduct a spiritual check-up:

1. Are you still experiencing the joy and energy of a relationship with Christ?

2. Have you moved beyond the initial acceptance of salvation to genuine growth in your faith? In what ways?

3. Take a few minutes to reflect on how your life has changed because of your trust in Christ.

Suggested Readings and Resources

Augustine. *The Confession: The Works of Saint Augustine: A Translation for the 21st Century*. Edited by John E. Potelle. Translated by Maria Boulding. Hyde Park, NY: New City Press, 2001.

Bonhoeffer, D. *The Cost of Discipleship*. New York: Simon & Schuster, 1995. First published in German (Nachfolge) in 1937.

Bridges, J. *The Pursuit of Holiness*. Colorado Springs: Navpress, 1996.

Bright, B. *Have You Heard of the Four Spiritual Laws?* Peachtree City, GA: New Life Publishers, 1993.

Colson, C. *Born Again*. Grand Rapids, MI: Fleming H. Revell, 1996.

Henrichsen, W. A. *Disciples Are Made, Not Born*. San Luis Obispo, CA: David C. Cook Publishing Company, 2002.

Lewis, C. S. *Mere Christianity*. San Francisco: Harper, 2001. First published in 1943 by MacMillan.

McDowell, J. *The New Evidence That Demands a Verdict*. Nashville: Nelson Reference, 1999.

Endnotes

1. The Barna Group. http://www.barna.org (accessed August 5, 2007).

2. "The Four Spiritual Laws" and scriptural references are from the Web page of Campus Crusade for Christ available online at http://www.crusade.org/downloads/article/resources/4sprituallaws.pdf (accessed August 5, 2007).

understanding the basics

the power of sanctification

*It is God's will that you should be sanctified . . . For God did
not call us to be impure, but to live a holy life.
Therefore, he who rejects this instruction does not reject
man but God, who gives you his Holy Spirit.*
(1 Thessalonians 4:3a, 7–8)

a church camp memory:
the men in black

I looked around at a group of men wearing plain black suits, Buddy Holly glasses, and retreaded wing tips. I had been duped—this "men's meeting" wasn't a breakfast. Instead, it was a 7 AM prayer meeting with a bunch of "holiness" preachers.

We were at a large ultra-conservative family camp in Frankfort, Indiana. The whole white-washed building affair was new to me—and one I nearly missed.

My jacked-up, souped-up black Gremlin pulled onto that campground and might as well have been a deer with a target for a birthmark. When I stepped out wearing a tank top, shorts, and sporting a cross between a mullet and a shag, the camp elders asked me to leave. I was a long-haired high school kid in a funny-looking car with extra-wide chrome wheels and, according to the preacher-turned-security guard, likely only interested in the girls.

Well, he was right about the last part. I knew a couple of them and noticed something different about them—a wholesomeness that distinguished them from the other girls at school. They didn't smoke pot, weren't running with loose guys, and were generally polite. And, some of my friends were there, like Phil. Although he had tricked me into going to a men's meeting, he was also among the group who caught me as I was pulling away from the camp. They convinced me to stay and convinced the temporary parish police patrol that I wasn't a criminal. This group of friends loaned me shirts with sleeves and long pants.

Phil wasted no time in pulling a fast one on me. He knew I'd be out of place with the camp elders at the men's meeting. He couldn't restrain himself.

He also pulled one of the funnier things I've seen in a religious service. We were all asked to kneel at the altar at the front of the expansive but simple tabernacle. Surrounded by Johnny-Cash-appareled preachers, I stayed quiet and hoped it would all pass quickly. As a non-Christian, prayer was a bit outside my comfort zone.

Then it began. The deep-voiced consensus leader asked, "Brother Smith, will you lead us to the throne of grace?"

In unison the men moved like a single dark cloak, removed their hats, and knelt on the cement floor around simple wooden altars that seemed to stretch to eternity. Brother Smith began, "Dear Heavenly Father, We beseech you . . ."

Way down on my left, a voice joined in—while Brother Smith was still praying—"Oh, Yes-a Lord-a . . .!" A third one piped in, "Oh, ah, Lord-a . . ." Before I knew it, I was in a room of chanting Charismatics at sunrise. That large, nearly empty tabernacle was full of loud voices.

"Yes, ah, Lord-a!"

"Oh, ah, Lord-a!"

"Thank ya, Lord-a!"

And then Phil, quiet up to this point, blurted out,

"Sold-a, to the man in blue-a!"

That was a memorable first encounter with leaders in a branch of Protestantism known for its "holiness" doctrines. I'm sure they thought that the long-haired transplant, not the short-haired choirboy Phil, had yelled the insensitive auctioneer comment. When the consensus leader began to pray aloud, somehow the rest of them knew to stop. I wasn't sure what God sounded like, but that voice was probably close. With his final "Amen," the meeting was over. I darted for the cafeteria and tried not to make eye contact with the men in black.

Ten years later, I returned to that same campground—no longer a longhair, but not dressed in black, either. One of the men from that auctioneer altar kidded me as I made my way to the platform— "Looky here," he said as he squeezed my cheek. "Who would have thought this? I think the Red Sea has parted again."

Through it all, these men in black introduced me to the "why" behind their austere actions—a deep desire to give every aspect of their lives to Christ. They told me that when people become saved, the Holy Spirit comes into their lives. As they grow in Christ, they come to a point at which they realize more fully what that new relationship means. At that point, they choose to become "entirely sanctified."

This chapter unpacks this notion in more detail. It also shows how one can become fully committed to Christ, sanctified for His purposes, by being or by not being legalistic.

Regardless of the cultural shifts, the biblical message and challenge to be set apart for Christ will speak to each generation. It'll take on different forms, and every generation will have those who appear legalistic and those who appear too socially liberal. Both groups read the same Bible and follow the same Lord.

Some of those black-cloaked preachers from that memorable tabernacle moment are now in heaven. Several of those who are still living have become my friends.

I realize now those altars that looked like they stretched from here to eternity—probably did.

understanding
the basics

the power of sanctification

 Consider the Source

It is God's will that you should be sanctified . . . For God did not call us to be impure, but to live a holy life. Therefore, he who rejects this instruction does not reject man but God, who gives you his Holy Spirit. (1 Thessalonians 4:3a, 7–8)

 Understand the Need

Be perfect, therefore, as your heavenly Father is perfect. (Matthew 5:48)

Since we have these promises, dear friends, let us purify ourselves from everything that contaminates body and spirit, perfecting holiness out of reverence for God. (2 Corinthians 7:1)

May God himself, the God of peace, sanctify you through and through. May your whole spirit, soul and body be kept blameless at the coming of our Lord Jesus Christ. The one

who calls you is faithful and he will do it. (1 Thessalonians
5:23–24)

Sanctification is God's Spirit at work in my mind, soul, spirit,
body—my entire life—changing my desires, thoughts, interests,
attitudes, and behavior. Keith Drury describes sanctification as how
"God transforms me into His Son's likeness."[1] Christians, like all
people, have human desires and areas of weakness. Many times
these desires get out of control and, as a result, we become self-
centered and self-gratifying rather than Christ-honoring. Although
we will always be influenced by human desires, through the process
of sanctification we can have power over those counterproductive
motivations: the power that comes by yielding to the leading, and
significant influence of the Holy Spirit. When we totally yield to the
Spirit, the potential for this deeper cleansing can occur in our lives.
This is God's provision for us to achieve victory over those desires
that often enslave our lives. We can be free, like Christ. We can be
Christlike!

God's Design for Sanctification

There is a considerable difference of opinion among various
Christian denominations about how sanctification occurs in the life of a
believer. The three predominant views of sanctification are as follows:

- **We are sanctified at the moment of conversion**. Those
  who ascribe to this view of sanctification hold that in
  God's eyes we are declared righteous and holy, even
  though our day-to-day conduct might not reflect holiness.

- **Sanctification is more than "appearing" righteous in
  God's eyes**. Under this view, sanctification is an actual
  transformation of one's nature by a gradual process of
  becoming more Christlike. However, advocates of this
  view also believe the fallen nature with which we are
  born prevents us from ever fully attaining the goal until
  we are made perfect after death.

- **Along with the gradual growth toward Christlikeness, we can experience a recognized time of "entire" sanctification—when a believer invites the Holy Spirit to take complete power over all areas of his or her life.** Christians go through three stages in this cleansing process: (1) **initial sanctification** at the time that we establish a personal relationship with Jesus Christ, (2) **gradual sanctification** as we grow in that relationship and are cleansed through the grace and love of Jesus Christ, and (3) **entire sanctification** that is exemplified by a complete and thorough surrender to the power of the Holy Spirit controlling every aspect of our lives.

We will explore this third view in greater detail below. Remember, however, this is but one explanation of sanctification. Although it is a logical conclusion from the Scriptures above, these same Scriptures are used to support other views.

Initial Sanctification

A Look at Your Own Life

Are you leading a spiritual life? Imagine that you're in a courtroom trial with God as the ultimate judge. One by one, familiar faces come forth to the witness stand—friends, coworkers, church members, teachers, and relatives. All are asked, "By word and deed, is the accused living a spiritual life?" In this courtroom, they answer directly to God. But in life, you do. What's your final answer?

—Dawn Brown

When we invite Jesus Christ into our hearts and lives, we experience a new birth—we are born again! God's divine power transforms and welcomes us as His newborn sons and daughters. At that very moment, the Holy Spirit comes to dwell in us and initiate a cleansing process in our lives. Like newborn infants, we are as alive (spiritually) as we ever will be; nonetheless, we are still immature and need to develop in order to actualize all of the spiritual potential that is given to us at the time of our new birth.

You, however, are controlled not by the sinful nature but by the Spirit, if the Spirit of God lives in you. And if anyone does not have the Spirit of Christ, he does not belong to Christ. But if Christ is in you, your body is dead because of sin, yet your spirit is alive because of righteousness. (Romans 8:9–10)

Even after this act of dedicating oneself to God, there is room for growth in love. God will continue to reveal areas of your life that can be shaped by His power and grace.

Until we all reach unity in the faith and in the knowledge of the Son of God and become mature, attaining to the whole measure of the fullness of Christ. (Ephesians 4:13)

In the classic book, *My Utmost for His Highest,* Oswald Chambers points out that choosing to pursue sanctification is not an easy path. It is one that should be taken seriously:

We take the term sanctification much too lightly. Are we prepared for what sanctification will cost? It will cost an intense narrowing of all our interests on earth, and an immense broadening of all our interests in God. Sanctification means intense concentration on God's point of view. It means every power of body, soul and spirit chained and kept for God's purpose only. Are we prepared for God to do in us all that He separated us for? And then after His work is done in us, are we prepared to separate ourselves to God even as Jesus did? "For their sakes I sanctify Myself." The reason some of us have not entered into the experience of sanctification is that we have not realized the meaning of sanctification from God's standpoint. Sanctification means being made one with Jesus so that the disposition that ruled Him will rule us. Are we prepared for what that will cost? It will cost everything that is not of God in us. Are we prepared to be caught up into the swing of this prayer of the apostle Paul's? Are we prepared to say—"Lord, make me as holy as You can make a sinner saved by grace"? Jesus has prayed that we might be one with Him as He is one with the Father. The one and only characteristic of the Holy Ghost in a man is a strong family likeness to Jesus Christ, and freedom from everything that is unlike Him. Are we prepared to set ourselves apart for the Holy Spirit's ministrations in us?[2]

As infants in Christ, it is crucial to have spiritual mentors who take on the responsibility of teaching us how to make Jesus Christ the core of our daily existence. We need to find people who can teach us about the beliefs of the faith and help us to begin practicing the disciplines of prayer and time in God's Word.

Gradual Sanctification

There is a time element involved in this important cleansing process. The Holy Spirit cleanses us, but we also must respond to His work in our lives. First, we must repent. We are to cease doing evil things and turn away from them. This is the process of putting off our "old self."

Since we have these promises, dear friends, let us purify ourselves from everything that contaminates body and spirit, perfecting holiness out of reverence for God. (2 Corinthians 7:1)

Do not lie to each other, since you have taken off your old self with its practices and have put on the new self, which is being renewed in knowledge in the image of its Creator. (Colossians 3:9—10)

As we make day-to-day decisions to be obedient to God, we should notice a transformation taking place in our lives. This transformation alters not only our patterns of behavior, but also the inner attitudes of our heart.

Think for a moment about the process of yielding your life to Jesus Christ. During that process you should begin to exercise

> ost of us have a number of years ahead of us, and we want them to be fulfilling and productive years. We can, however, live for many years without purpose and fulfillment, unless we are completely yielded to Christ and allow him full control of our daily activities. This does not mean a drab dull life of drudgery, with no thrills. Each new day with Christ is an exciting adventure.
>
> Charlie Riggs
> *Learning to Walk with God*[3]

"Lordship"—making Jesus the Lord of your heart and your life. What are some of the current evidences of that process in your life?

Christians often leave worship services and motivational Christian events feeling uplifted, energized, and inspired. Then, after a period of time, they feel a familiar pulling from within to return to their sinful lifestyle. This force is more than "human nature." It is an intruding force that uses our own nature against us. Paul asserts that Christians can have victory over this bent to sinning.

If we have been united with him like this in his death, we will certainly also be united with him in his resurrection. For we know the our old self was crucified with him so that the body of sin might be done away with, that we should no longer be slaves to sin—because anyone who has died has been freed from sin. (Romans 6:5–7)

The mind of a sinful man is death, but the mind controlled by the Spirit is life and peace; the sinful mind is hostile to God. It does not submit to God's law, nor can it do so. Those controlled by the sinful nature cannot please God. You, however, are controlled not by the sinful nature but by the Spirit, if the Spirit of God lives in you. (Romans 8:6–9)

John Wesley, the founder of Methodism, often declared that the essence of a sanctified (holy) life is outlined in 1 Thessalonians 5:16–18. Consider the same source that Wesley consulted:

Be joyful always; pray continually; give thanks in all circumstances, for this is God's will for you in Christ Jesus. (1 Thessalonians 5:16–18)

Wesley's simple outline for living the holy life:

- Verse 16 — Be joyful always.

- Verse 17 — Pray continually.

- Verse 18 — Give thanks in all circumstances, for this is God's will for you in Christ Jesus.

Can you share the Apostle Paul's personal mission statement?

Not that I have already obtained all this, or have already been made perfect, but I press on to take hold of that for which Christ Jesus took hold of me . . . One thing I do: Forgetting what is behind and straining toward what is ahead, I press on toward the goal to win the prize for which God has called me heavenward in Christ Jesus. (Philippians 3:12–13)

Entire Consecration

Sanctification Made Simple

Sanctification addresses the entire work of transformation in our lives by the Holy Spirit from the moment we are born again until we are glorified at death. The ultimate end of the Spirit's work is to restore the full image of God in us, making us like Christ.

When the Spirit takes residence in our lives, He begins the process of transforming our attitudes, interests, and actions, while confronting us with a principle of selfishness and sin that persists stubbornly in us. Through our act of total consecration and faith, the Spirit conquers this principle and enables us to love God entirely, to live in obedience to His revealed will and to serve others in love. Over time, as we continually submit to the Spirit, He deepens our love, increases our knowledge of God's will, and brings us into greater conformity with Christ until we reach final sanctification in death.

—Chris Bounds

As Christians, we should be looking forward and striving for a "full" act of cleansing. The human response that makes this a possibility is the conscious and purposeful act of consecration (or spiritual surrender) of our lives to God. The Apostle Paul prayed:

May the Lord make your love increase and overflow for each other and for everyone else, just as ours does for you. May he strengthen your hearts so that you will be blameless and holy in the presence of our God and Father when our Lord Jesus comes with all his holy ones. (1 Thessalonians 3:12–13)

Paul also admonished his fellow believers:

Therefore, I urge you, brothers, in view of God's mercy, to offer your bodies as living sacrifices, holy and pleasing to God—this is your spiritual act of worship. Do not conform any longer to the pattern of this world, but be transformed by the renewing of your mind. Then you will be able to test and approve what God's will is—his good, pleasing and perfect will. (Romans 12:1–2)

On Connecting

It was early one Sunday morning, and I was standing on a mountain in the middle of a cloud. I had just awakened to the city of Quito, Ecuador—hundreds of miles away from anything familiar to me and hundreds of miles from all that I considered mine. Even so, in that moment I felt an acute sense of belonging, of *home* like I had never felt before and have not felt since.

As I stood in my strange surroundings with wind in my hair and cloud at my feet, I was suddenly aware of the hugeness of the earth on which I existed. I tried to picture myself on the planet's scale, and my eyes widened and then blinked in recognition of my smallness, my insignificance. Then, just before my inferiority complex could kick in, I was reminded of the God who created and ruled both my world and the world of this beautiful unfamiliarity. I imagined Him looking out across His creation, looking through the atmosphere and past the deserts, looking over the oceans and around the mountains—looking directly at me where I stood in the cloud. That was the moment when I first felt redemption.

A person does not understand sanctification until he understands some of his own smallness. Unless we can grasp how much of a stoop it was for God to come down to our level, we will not appreciate His redemption. And until we can make that connection between God's grace and our need for it, we will not feel the need for sanctification. Knowing that God recognizes our value despite our smallness is the thing that compels us to obey Him. It makes us want to be bigger than we are where we stand.

—Lisa Velthouse

 FAQ

Q. How can sanctification specifically help a Christian?

A. Bitterness and unforgiving attitudes can be conquered. The Apostle Paul gives some specific examples as to how:

> *Do not let any unwholesome talk come out of your mouths, but only what is helpful for building others up according to their needs, that it may benefit those who listen. And do not grieve the Holy Spirit of God, with whom you were sealed for the day of redemption. Get rid of all bitterness, rage and anger, brawling and slander, along with every form of malice. Be kind and compassionate to one another, forgiving each other, just as in Christ God forgave you. Be imitators of God, therefore, as dearly loved children and live a life of love, just as Christ loved us and gave himself up for us as a fragrant offering and sacrifice to God.* (Ephesians 4:29—5:2)

Q. What exactly is the role of the Holy Spirit here on earth?

A. Jesus Christ's recorded statement provides the best answer to this question:

I tell you the truth, anyone who has faith in me will do what I have been doing. He will do even greater things than these, because I am going to the Father. And I will do whatever you ask in my name, so that the Son may bring glory to the Father. You may ask me for anything in my name, and I will do it . . . And I will ask the Father, and he will give you another Counselor to be with you forever— the Spirit of truth. The world cannot accept him, because it neither sees him nor knows him. But you know him, for he lives with you and will be in you. I will not leave you as orphans; I will come to you. Before long, the world will not see me anymore, but you will see me. Because I live, you also will live. On that day you will realize that I am in my Father, and you are in me, and I am in you. Whoever has my commands and obeys them, he is the one who loves me. He who loves me will be loved by my Father, and I too will love him and show myself to him . . . All this I have spoken while still with you. But the Counselor, the Holy Spirit, whom the Father will send in my name, will teach you all things and will remind you of everything I have said to you. Peace I leave with you; my peace I give you. I do not give to you as the world gives. Do not let your hearts be troubled and do not be afraid.

You heard me say, "I am going away and I am coming back to you." If you loved me, you would be glad that I am going to the Father, for the Father is greater than I. I have told you now before it happens, so that when it does happen you will believe. I will not speak with you much longer, for the prince of this world [the devil] *is coming. He has no hold on me, but the world must learn that I love the Father and that I do exactly what my Father has commanded me.* (John 14:12–21, 25–31; see also John 16:5–16)

Reaction and Reflection

1. Have you moved beyond experiencing God's forgiveness (salvation) and begun this process of growing in Christlikeness?

2. Have you offered yourself as a "living sacrifice" to God? What are the evidences that you have made that commitment?

3. When you think about the process of sanctification, what types of applications can you make to your own spiritual condition?

4. Do you dare to believe that the Holy Spirit dwelling in your life can transform you into a person who demonstrates perfect love for God and others? What verses of Scripture support your beliefs?

Suggested Readings and Resources

Bridges, J. *The Pursuit of Holiness*. Colorado Springs: Navpress, 1996.

Christenson, L. *The Renewed Mind*. New York: Walker and Company, 2002.

DeNeff, S. *Whatever Became of Holiness?* Indianapolis: Wesleyan Publishing House, 1995.

———. *More Than Forgiveness: A Contemporary Call to Holiness Based on the Life of Jesus Christ*. Indianapolis: Wesleyan Publishing House, 2002.

Drury, K. *Holiness for Ordinary People*. Indianapolis: Wesleyan Publishing House, 1983.

———. *Spiritual Disciplines for Ordinary People*. Indianapolis: Wesleyan Publishing House, 1991.

Foster, R. J. *Celebration of Discipline*. San Francisco: Harper Collins, 1998.

Getz, G. A. *The Measure of a Man*. Glendale, CA: Regal Books, 1974.

Getz, G. A., and Getz, E.A. *The Measure of a Woman*. Ventura, CA: Regal Books, 1984.

Ortberg, J. *The Life You've Always Wanted*. Grand Rapids, MI: Zondervan Publishing House, 1997.

Riggs, C. *Learning to Walk with God*. Minneapolis: World Wide Publications, 1988.

Smith, T. L. *Called Unto Holiness*. Kansas City: Beacon Hill Press, 1962.

Wesley, J. *A Plain Account of Christian Perfection*. Kansas City: Beacon Hill Press, 1966.

White, J. *Daring to Draw Near: Prayers That Help Us Know Who God Is*. Carol Stream, IL: Tyndale House Publishers, 2000.

Endnotes

1. Keith Drury, commenting on 2 Corinthians 3:18. Used by permission.

2. Oswald Chambers. "February 8," in *My Utmost for His Highest*. © 1935 by Dodd Mead & Co., renewed © 1963 by the Oswald Chambers Publications Assn., Ltd., and is used by permission of Discovery House Publishers, Grand Rapids, MI. Available online at http://www.myutmost.org (accessed August 5, 2007).

3. Charlie Riggs, *Learning to Walk with God*. (Minneapolis: World Wide Publications, 1988), 40.

faith
in action

christian morality and sexual purity

*I have hidden your word in my heart that
I might not sin against you.*
(Psalm 119:11)

a buck creek memory:
running in the wrong direction

O nly once in my lackluster track career did I pass our school's best runner—but everyone did, head on. When the gun sounded for the 1500, he ran in the wrong direction. Our track star's magnetic smile had masked his addiction, the kind of speed he didn't need.

The event was surrealistic. The race occurred while students (dressed in the scraggly clothes that marked the seventies) whistled and yelled. At the starting line, the surfer-looking star had us all laughing. At that moment, we all knew that he was untouchable. He had dominated every race, every meet. It was a windy day, and his flowing quasi-mullet made him appear even more relaxed.

He was over six feet tall. I was an anemic 5'8". His long legs had muscles that separated with every step. My legs looked like two strings hanging from my belt. He had a *GQ* face with a strong jaw. I had more of a DQ look.

He was standing with folded arms, still chatting when the gun sounded. His confidence was unnerving. I rounded the first turn and caught a glimpse of him running in his characteristic style on the other end of the track—running the other way. We thought he was joking. As he ran through us, he seemed unusually happy, but noticeably disoriented.

Concern supplanted humor.

He circled the cinder track before the teachers could stop him. The race continued: our feet were moving but our heads were spinning. The image of adults scampering to protect our friend from himself was alarming. It's a sad bookmark from my Buck Creek days. I wish I could offer a happy ending to this story, but that was how it ended—a misguided freshman who never returned to organized sports.

I can't remember who won that race because everyone's attention was focused on the loser. He had broken a rule that disqualified him from participating in track and school for a season—but for him, seasonal became permanent.

I'm now 45, and have just witnessed another individual running in the wrong direction—a gay Episcopal priest. He, too, looked confident. Perhaps most unnerving of all is that when he approached a head-on collision with the traditional church, he had 62 bishops running with him.

Before the gun sounded, a group of people told him it was okay to run contrary to the established religious rules, the orthodox teachings of Christianity. Somehow, his homosexual lifestyle helped to blur the distinction between constitutional rights and religious rites. At some point, his coaches and mentors were taken in by his charisma, failed to separate personality from principle, and slighted the latter. Long before he stepped into the public arena, the rules were challenged. In time, they were ignored.

Anyone can go to a track and run clockwise, head-on into the pack, but if you want to be a part of the universal sport of track and field, you'll be disqualified. A group, whether two or two million, might opt for a different direction. Maybe they're tired of watching people always running right and leaning left.

The Episcopal Church, USA, has the prerogative to start an organization separate from orthodox Christianity, like *Slamball* and *X-Games* among sports. The question is not whether those involved in the decision to commission a gay bishop are well meaning, or whether the priest is competent. The question is whether they have violated standards basic to established Christianity.

In the mid-1990s, I began writing sections of this book after fielding hundreds of student questions about the basics of Christianity. A rather clear thread in the Bible is a call to refrain from immorality—which includes homosexuality (Romans 1). Likewise, the Bible is replete with stipulations for pastors to be above reproach morally. The recent decision to commission a gay bishop disregards, if you will, the "rule book" of orthodox Christianity. The term "orthodox" comes from the Greek words "straight" (orth) and "opinion" (doxa), and orthodoxy came to mean sound teachings recognized by the established Church. In a layperson's terms, orthodoxy means straight teaching from the Bible (*see the Glossary*).

The Episcopals' opinion isn't straight from the Bible. Their leaders are headed in a different direction than that of orthodox teaching. The two are hitting head-on. In a misguided effort to become more relevant in the short run, they risk becoming irrelevant in the long run.

Instead of mulletted youths cheering from the stands, 62 Episcopal bishops are taking unorthodox stands. It's okay to proclaim "love" and to endorse "tolerance," but not to take them to "an unwarranted extreme"—the essence of all heresy. One of the 45 dissenting Episcopal bishops warned that "the unity of this house will be shattered forever." At the same Episcopal meeting (5 August 2003), the gay priest, Rev. Gene Robinson, claimed that God is no longer in a "tiny box," and that gays and lesbians are now assured that the church loves them. This faulty logic assumes a clerical vote somehow changes God's constitution—that the church could not show love to gays and lesbians without a non-biblical sanctioning of a gay bishop.

The same Bible that underpins orthodoxy calls Christians to fight the good fight and run the good race. The Episcopal Church, USA, has picked a different fight, and is running a different race. In this age of relativism, perhaps some Episcopal priests will revise the old spiritual and sing, "We've got good reason to be happy and gay, the Bishops took all the rules away."

I ran track in college but never won a single race. However, I always ran in the right direction. To do otherwise was illogical.

When the gun sounds to start church this weekend, ask the simple question: "Are we running in the right direction?" If not, "What's the name of this new race?" The name "orthodox Christianity" is already taken.[1]

This chapter helps to articulate the moral message of Scripture. There is no doubt about which way to run when it comes to sexual purity.

faith

in action

christian morality and sexual purity

 ## Consider the Source

Similarly, encourage the young men to be self-controlled. In everything set them an example by doing what is good. In your teaching show integrity, seriousness and soundness of speech that cannot be condemned, so that those who oppose you may be ashamed because they have nothing bad to say about us. (Titus 2:6–8)

So in everything, do to others what you would have them do to you, for this sums up the Law and the Prophets. (Matthew 7:12)

 ## Understand the Need

How would you describe the moral climate of the American culture? As time passes, it becomes dramatically easier to observe blatant examples of societal tolerance for immoral behaviors and practices. Stated differently, it is reasonable to propose that we live in a culture that encourages and even rewards the proliferation of immorality. Consider some examples from our recent past:

- Various large cities have experimented with a "sexual combat zone" where the usual legal standards applicable to prostitution and other sex-related crimes are not enforced.

- In several regional locations across the country, homosexual behavior is blatantly displayed and fully accepted as part of the local culture.

- The Episcopal Church, USA, confirmed an openly gay bishop, a direct contradiction of biblical standards.

- In various communities in Nevada, prostitution has been legalized and provides a significant contribution to the local economy.

- The state of Vermont (with many others poised to follow) has legalized "civil unions" that have facilitated the reality of same-sex marriages.

- Internet sites that cater to a variety of perverted and immoral sexual preferences have proliferated.

- A press release from the Sexuality Information and Education Council of the United States (SIECUS) reveals that:

"Over 850 of America's religious leaders, to date, have endorsed the Religious Declaration on Sexual Morality, Justice, and Healing, a new progressive statement that affirms that sexuality is one of God's most fulfilling gifts and outlines a new paradigm for sexual morality that does not discriminate on the basis of age, marital status, or sexual orientation. Endorsers of the declaration represent a broad range of faith traditions and include two denomination presidents, 15 seminary presidents and academic deans, theologians from more than 32 seminaries, and 14 bishops . . . The Religious Declaration on Sexual Morality, Justice, and Healing calls for full inclusion of women and sexual minorities . . . and the blessing of same sex unions."[2]

- In June 2003, the United States Supreme Court provided a de facto endorsement of homosexual behavior.

- In the fall of 2003, the city of New York opened a high school for gay, lesbian, and bisexual high school students.

- Television, radio, and movies continue to exploit and graphically depict various sexual and immoral behavior patterns. Most recently, media programming has taken a turn toward "reality" programs. These shows often chronicle sexual behavior and glorify choices and behavior leading to premarital sex, adultery, and homosexual relationships.

Christ and Culture

This generation has witnessed an abundance of deception and lies. Many spiritual leaders have failed morally, and political leaders have lied openly. Mass media continues to blur the lines of entertainment and reality: they are nearly indistinguishable and often appear one and the same. What is seen from ABC to MTV has in effect become the window to the world—one which is void of absolutes and morals.

It has become our Christian cause to understand the culture, to identify it, to see through it, and then to expose it for all to see. We can no longer try to compete with it or manipulate it to our advantage. We must stand on the Truth that exposes it and on that Rock stake our claim. Christ must be preached as the end and not just a beginning. He must be identified as our only hope and not just another option. To be like Him is the challenge that we must preach. We must not, we will not, see Him as a choice like just another TV channel. Christ is the One who gives us distinction, identity, purpose, and place. And above all else, He is the only one who gives everlasting life—something our culture can't compete with because it has no supply of it.

The call is to be authentic, to be real, to be free, not in our ability to create or manipulate, but in complete faith, believing that only through total abandonment will He produce the life that we seek.

—Charlie Alcock

These are only a few of the illustrations that can be used to demonstrate the ongoing moral decline of our nation. This concern was never more evident, however, than in 1998 when the President of the United States faced impeachment due to allegations of sexual misconduct in the White House. The national news media and the American public wrestled with the question of whether marital infidelity was a matter of public or private concern. Although Congress and the majority of the American public did not consider his actions sufficient cause to warrant removal from office, there was strong condemnation of his behavior and a pervasive sense that President Clinton's sexual conduct had seriously eroded the credibility of his office. It only stands to reason that Christians, followers of the only morally perfect man to walk on this earth, should at least expect biblical injunctions to be as demanding as those expectations placed on the nation's leader. Although only God, Bill Clinton, and his accusers know the true and correct verdict, the nation imposed varying moral standards on the Congressional hearings. Fortunately, Christ's guidelines are more specific. They also precisely define moral standards and immoral behavior. In this chapter, we will examine some of these commands and some specific strategies that we can use to remain obedient to God's plan and will.

The Command

God is the Master Designer and Creator of the universe. As part of His master plan, He established guidelines for us to follow. The high calling of being Christlike is reflected by a desire to be pure in the sight of God. One of the most important challenges that we all face on a daily basis is moral decision making, particularly in the area of sexual involvements. Both our inner peace and public testimony are strongly affected by the manner in which we deal with our sexual desires, thoughts, energies, and involvements. God designed sex as an enriching aspect of marriage. The Bible clearly delineates that sex before marriage (referred to as fornication) is a sin. Sex outside of a marriage relationship (referred to as adultery) is also labeled as sinful behavior. The sexual command is an instruction from God intended to be in our best interest for our fulfillment and well-being.

If it is God's plan for you to marry, sex can become a vibrant and exciting physical expression within the context of that relationship. In a marriage relationship, "sex" and "sin" are not synonymous. But for unmarried Christians, the Holy Spirit will help you to keep sex in its proper place—it is displeasing in the sight of God before and outside of marriage. For all people, their sense of what is right and their consciences help to remind them of these moral boundaries. Some Bible teachers propose that the Holy Spirit works through these human dimensions in both Christians and non-Christians to convict them of sin and/or to challenge them to be obedient to God's laws.

> *Indeed, when Gentiles, who do not have the law, do by nature things required by the law, they are a law for themselves, even though they do not have the law, since they show that the requirements of the law are written on their hearts, their consciences also bearing witness, and their thoughts now accusing, now even defending them.* (Romans 2:14–15)

> *But the fruit of the Spirit is love, joy, peace, patience, kindness, goodness, faithfulness, gentleness and self-control. Against such things there is no law.* (Galatians 5:22–23)

The Myth of Invisibility

There is an unfortunate human tendency to believe that we can sin "in private," away from the vision of others, and that these sins are a private matter. The nineteenth-century English historian Baron Thomas Babington McCauley observed, "The measure of a man's real character is what he would do if he knew he would never be found out."[3] This observation encourages us to live in a manner that promotes a consistency between what we do in private (e.g., our private thoughts, things we do when "no one else is watching") and our public persona. For the Christian, this issue goes deeper. For in God's Word we are told this:

> *But if you fail to do this, you will be sinning against the Lord; and you may be sure that your sin will find you out.* (Numbers 32:23)

> ## "Right" from the Start
>
> The year after I graduated from college, I worked as an admissions counselor for my alma mater. While staying in hotels, I used the school credit card to make personal calls. I justified this in my mind, saying, "Hey, I'm doing this for them. I've earned it." Well, as you might imagine, the Holy Spirit began to convict me and one day in prayer I knew that I was stealing from the school and that I needed to make restitution. I estimated how much I had spent, added to it to be sure, and went to the business office to confess and make right what I had stolen. I cried and felt totally humiliated, but the amazing thing was that with the confession and restitution came great peace and freedom. That fall I learned that it is better to do what's right from the start—it makes life so much easier!
>
> —Judy Huffman

In other words, God sees and knows about our sinful behavior even when we somehow manage to hide those behaviors from our friends, coworkers, and loved ones. Even when we are able to elude "being caught" or seen, all of our thoughts and actions are known to God.

According to Scripture, sinning is a matter of the heart. When our hearts are pure and driven by the power of the Holy Spirit, we live in obedience to God's commands. When our hearts are driven by human desires, we pursue those things that are displeasing to God. In a sense, our sins are evidenced in our hearts:

If we had forgotten the name of our God or spread out our hands to a foreign god, would not God have discovered it, since he knows the secrets of the heart? (Psalm 44:20–21)

I have hidden your word in my heart that I might not sin against you. (Psalm 119:11)

Who can say, "I have kept my heart pure; I am clean and without sin?" (Proverbs 20:9)

Granted, our sinful nature will often tend to lead us in directions that we should not travel. Consider the following steps that can help lead us away from engaging in sinful behavior—public and private—that is displeasing to God.

Five Steps to Conquering Temptation

No temptation has seized you except what is common to man. And God is faithful; he will not let you be tempted beyond what you can bear. But when you are tempted, he will also provide a way out so that you can stand up under it. (1 Corinthians 10:13)

We can take great comfort from this passage. We serve a God who is fully aware of the challenges that we face in the area of temptation. Additionally, God has promised to provide a means of escape for us during those times when we are confronted even with our most challenging temptations. In this process, however, God's provision of a "way out" also requires that we take advantage of the opportunity and follow God's leading and direction in response to temptation. If Christ instructs us to overcome temptations, then we need to look into His teachings for direction. Several specific strategies outlined in God's Word will assist you in conquering temptations.

Recognize a Weakness

First, we must be willing to recognize that we all have areas of weakness and temptation in our lives. We must name these areas of weakness and acknowledge that they are part of the challenge we face as we try to live closer to God. We can be encouraged because God is ready and willing to help us overcome these areas of difficulty. Isn't it heartening to know that God fully understands the reality of your temptations and weaknesses and that He is interested in being part of the solution?

What areas of challenge and temptation are interfering with your relationship with God and your desire to move closer to Him on a daily basis?

Keep a Clean Mind

Make a conscious effort to keep a clean mind. It is God's desire that we rid ourselves of those thoughts that will lead us into temptation.

Blessed are they whose ways are blameless, who walk according to the law of the LORD. Blessed are they who keep his statutes and seek Him with all their heart. They do nothing wrong; they walk in his ways. You have laid down precepts that are to be fully obeyed. Oh, that my ways were steadfast in obeying your decrees! Then I would not be put to shame when I consider all your commands. I will praise you with an upright heart as I learn your righteous laws. I will obey your decrees; do not utterly forsake me. How can a young man keep his way pure? By living according to your word. I seek you with all my heart; do not let me stray from your commands. I have hidden your word in my heart that I might not sin against you. Praise be to you, O LORD; teach me your decrees. With my lips I recount all the laws that come from your mouth. I rejoice in following your statutes as one rejoices in great riches. I meditate on your precepts and consider your ways. I delight in your decrees; I will not neglect your word. (Psalm 119:1–16)

Finally, brothers, whatever is true, whatever is noble, whatever is right, whatever is pure, whatever is lovely, whatever is admirable—if anything is excellent or praiseworthy—think about such things. (Philippians 4:8)

In the verses above, we are given several key actions to perform as a means of protecting our minds from the contamination of temptation and sin. These verses describe the lifestyle and thought patterns of an individual who has chosen to pursue holiness in every aspect of life. The mind is the gateway to this process.

Thomas Lickona has described the process of character development as a three-step process: (1) knowing the good, (2) loving the good, and (3) doing the good.[4] This progression moves from the mind (cognitively knowing what is right and what is wrong), to the heart (making a commitment from the inner core of your heart and soul to do what is right), to the actions of our daily life (how we follow through on our beliefs and commitments). From this scenario, we can readily see the starting point for either a life of character or a life that moves in directions of immoral behavior.

In the book *Navigating Toward Home*, Craig Peters describes the relationship between the landscapes of our minds and the destiny of our lifestyles:

> The King James Version says, "Gird up the loins of your mind." What does this imply? To gird up your loins indicates getting ready for service, activity, or labor at any time or place. To loosen the loins denotes giving way to idleness or laziness. What condition have the loins of your mind been in—watchfulness or laziness? You see, if we're not allowing the Lord to prepare our minds for Christ-like action, then someone or something else will come along and prepare it for another type of action, guaranteed not to bring us closer to God. (See Ephesians 2:2) . . . We must gain and maintain control of our thought life. How do we begin that process? First Peter 1:14 tells us: "Do not conform to the evil desires you had when you lived in ignorance." To be conformed means to agree in thought or idea. God calls us to be different from what we were before we accepted Christ. The best way to stay on course is to gird our minds with the Word of Truth so we will know in advance the correct course of action . . . Loose thoughts lead to loose lifestyles that prepare you to go in a different way than you desire.[5]

Endeavor today to keep a clean mind . . . with God's help.

Starve the Source

Love must be sincere. Hate what is evil; cling to what is good. (Romans 12:9)

If you know the source of your temptation, stay away from it as much as possible. Whether these temptations are certain people, the Internet, particular situations or places, television programs or movies—whatever they may be, make plans to avoid the circumstances that feed your temptations. Consider, for example, television programming during the "family hour" from 8 to 9 PM. A recent study that examined the content of television programming during that time slot revealed the following results:

- The overall ratio of sex-outside-marriage to sex-within-marriage was 3.6 to 1.
- 31% of the programs contained at least one reference to sexual intercourse.
- Of the 86 family-hour shows rated "PG" (i.e., programs that are supposedly appropriate for everyone except young children), 35% contained sexual references and 49% contained obscenities.[6]

It would appear that the media is intent on pushing the limits to an extreme: "Shock jock" radio programs, "reality programming," music videos, talk shows that cater to a celebration of outrageous behaviors, magazines featuring highly sexualized content, and questionable standards for the rating of movies—these are daily events in all forms of the media. A reasonable follow-up question in response to this data would be, "How do Christians typically respond to media programming that would be considered objectionable based on the presence of sexual references or obscenities?" The Barna Research Group addressed this question with the following results:

- "Churched" individuals were more likely to choose not to watch a particularly objectionable movie or video than their "unchurched" counterparts (22% compared with 7% respectively).
- "Churched" individuals were more likely to choose to turn off a television program they were watching because

it conflicted with their personal values when compared with their "unchurched" counterparts (47% compared with 34% respectively).

- "Unchurched" adults were more likely to have viewed "adult-only" content on the Internet (19% compared with 8% respectively).

- There was no significant difference between "churched" and "unchurched" individuals in regard to watching a movie or video that contained explicit sexual images. About one in every five adults had done so in the past week.[7]

This data can be viewed from two different perspectives. First, there is a strong tendency to immediately take the position that Christians (or "churched" individuals in the language of the Barna study) are doing "better" than non-Christians in many of these areas. That should be our expectation. The second perspective, however, relates to the habits of Christians in relation to God's standard of behavior, which is our model. Based on those two perspectives, take a fresh look at the data presented in the study described above. What are your impressions? What are your personal practices in the following areas?

- Television programs that depict or contain sexual content, questionable values, or images

- Questionable or inappropriate Web sites on the Internet

- Movies that depict or contain sexual content, questionable values, or images

- Books and magazines that depict or contain sexual content, questionable values, or images

- People and places that encourage you to engage in activities that would be displeasing to God

Starve the source of your temptations.

Follow the Pattern of Christ

As Christians, we have been given the ultimate example for living: the life of Christ. It is helpful and valuable to study the life of Christ and to pattern our actions accordingly.

I have set you an example that you should do as I have done for you. (John 13:15)

Your attitude should be the same as that of Christ Jesus. (Philippians 2:5)

Part of the process for building our relationship with Christ and living closer to Him on a daily basis is dealing effectively and biblically with our sin. Any sin has an effect on your relationship with Christ, but persistent or habitual sexual sins can seriously hinder or even sever this relationship more easily than most other sins. The Bible instructs us to walk in the ever-brightening light of God's favor. To keep in step with these commands, the Bible describes in a direct manner the effects and impact of sexual temptation and sins:

Avoid it, do not travel on it; turn from it and go on your way. For they cannot sleep till they do evil; they are robbed of slumber till they make someone fall. They eat the bread of wickedness and drink the wine of violence. The path of righteousness is like the first gleam of dawn, shining ever brighter till the full light of day. But the way of the wicked is like deep darkness; they do not know what makes them stumble. My son, pay attention to what I say; listen closely to my words. (Proverbs 4:15–20)

Being innocent of sexual sins makes it so much easier to love Christ with all your "heart, soul and mind":

Jesus replied: "'Love the Lord your God with all your heart and with all your soul and with all your mind.' This is the first and greatest commandment. And the second is like it:

'Love your neighbor as yourself.' All the Law and the Prophets hang on these two commandments." (Matthew 22:37–40)

As we look at the example of Christ, we also notice that He continually interacted with God the Father through prayer and frequent reference to the Holy Scriptures. This part of "following the pattern of Christ" invites us to spend time communicating with God in prayer and by studying the Word. Through these means we gain better insights into God's direction and plan for our lives, His expectations for our behavior, and the help and insight of the Holy Spirit.

Follow the pattern of Christ.

Be Accountable

Spiritual growth and the process of defending ourselves against the temptation of sin should not be a solitary experience. We were built by God to be relational, relying on one another for encouragement, support, and accountability. As you struggle with sin, it is always helpful to find another person you trust to hold you accountable for your behavior and your commitments. An "accountability partner" can provide you with support, assistance, and honest feedback.

In the book *How Good People Make Tough Choices,* Rushworth Kidder suggests three strategies for making good decisions that relate to the principle of accountability.[8] He suggests that when we must choose whether or not a behavior is appropriate, we should perform the following three tests:

The "Front Page Test"

How would I feel if my friends and family saw a story about me engaging in this behavior?

The "Mom Test"

How would I feel if my mom (or some other person in my life that I respect and admire) knew about my choice to engage in this behavior?

The "Stench Test"

Does this choice "stink"? Do I just simply know that this choice is wrong for me?

These tests provide us with a means for thinking about the choices we make every day.

Dating and Relationships

The maintenance of proper heterosexual relationships takes varying amounts of energy. When such a relationship develops into romance, at whatever level, the focus on what is "proper" should not be lost—but magnified. The biblical command to stay pure and to be good examples for "outsiders" (i.e., non-Christians) applies to all areas of morality and ethics. However, history, numerous biblical examples and references, and contemporary events remind us that the world is influenced by, or is critical of, the cross-gender actions of Christians. If and when you date, develop relationships that are spiritually sound. The following suggestions might help:

1. Have open discussions about feelings, including guilt; if someone does not feel free to discourse, then that particular relationship is definitely suspect. (Proverbs 4:23)

2. Insist on mutual agreement of moral standards: God's thoughts above yours—consult the Scriptures.

3. Plan your dates; prevent or eliminate the routine of long periods of idle time together if you are struggling with the physical aspect of your relationship.

4. Pray together often, especially about keeping the right perspective on physical involvement.

5. Remember, you want your dates and closest friends to be Christians—individuals seeking the mind of Christ. (1 Corinthians 15:33; 2 Corinthians 6:14)

6. As a relationship begins to get serious, plan joint times to read a good book on morals, dating, or a related subject.

Modern culture endorses and supports certain ritual behaviors related to male-female relationships. Under the general category of "dating," young men and women follow age-old traditions of attending events together, "going with" one another (i.e., a communication of some level of commitment to each other), becoming engaged to be married, and, ultimately, getting married. A variety of decisions can occur during this process, among them these:

- Decisions about faithfulness to one another
- Decisions about sexual involvement
- Decisions about continuing or discontinuing the relationship
- Decisions about whether or not to "get serious" about marriage
- Decisions about when to terminate a dating relationship
- Decisions about whether or not to "live together"
- Decisions to work toward understanding what is important in a relationship

For Christians and non-Christians, these are important issues. For the believer in Jesus Christ, however, other issues go beyond these traditional concerns of dating relationships. Each of the questions and issues above must be considered in light of biblical truths. Just "feeling good about things" is not enough. For the Christian, consideration must also be given to building God into the center of the relationship. This may include praying together, discussions of spiritual matters, decision making based upon spiritual and biblical principles, participation in worship and church attendance as a couple, participation in biblically oriented counseling on relationships, and conscious decisions to abstain from sex before marriage. In a sense, God becomes a key third member of the relationship. As we have been told in God's Word: "A cord of three strands is not quickly broken" (Ecclesiastes 4:12). Make God the third cord in your relationship.

What, then, are some biblical guidelines for dating relationships? Joshua Harris offers the following suggestions:

1. Guard your heart and be selective about how and where you give away your affections (Proverbs 4:23).

2. Be careful about the company that you keep, as we tend to act like the people with whom we associate (1 Corinthians 15:33).

3. Christians should only date other Christians (2 Corinthians 6:14). We certainly will have many friends and associate with many people who are not Christians. It is felt, however, that dating and marriage relationships—the closest personal relationships that we may ever have—should only be with other Christians.

4. Is it really love? (1 Corinthians 13:4–7).[9]

In the book *I Kissed Dating Goodbye* by Joshua Harris, the following questions are offered for determining whether a relationship is the "real thing":

- Is your relationship characterized by humility?
- Are you never rude to each other?
- Are you not self-seeking?
- Are you not easily angered with each other?
- Do you keep no record of wrongs?
- Are you truthful with each other?
- Do you protect each other?

These are the qualities of love according to the Bible. Have you found them in your relationships?

Charlie Riggs
Learning to Walk with God[10]

Here is a quick reference list related to the issues of dating, sexual behavior, and relationships, along with corresponding messages from God's Word:

• Person to date	Galatians 5:19–23; Psalm 1:1-6; Proverbs 31:10–13
• Dating non-Christians	2 Corinthians 6:14–18
• Getting a date	1 Peter 3:3–4; Proverbs 3:5–6
• How to date	Romans 13:14
• How to treat my date	Philippians 2:3–4
• Dressing for dates	1 Timothy 2:9–10; 1 Peter 3:3–4
• Guarding my reputation	Proverbs 22:1
• Quality of relationship	Psalm 34:3; Matthew 6:33
• Saying no	Colossians 4:6
• Where to go on dates	2 Corinthians 8:21; Romans 14:13b
• Physical limits	1 Corinthians 5:1–13; 1 Thessalonians 4:1–8; Proverbs 6:27–29; Matthew 5:27–28
• Response to roaming hands	1 Corinthians 6:18–20; 1 Peter 2:11
• Response to a girl's come-on	Genesis 39:7–12; 2 Timothy 2:22
• Public display of affection	Proverbs 4:23
• Emotional attachment	Proverbs 4:23
• Saying "I love you"	1 Peter 1:22
• Showing love	1 Corinthians 13:4–8
• Waiting until marriage	1 Corinthians 6:18–20
• Purpose for dating	Ephesians 4:1–3[11]

On Rippling

We make hundreds of thousands of decisions in our lifetime. Some are momentary at best; we forget them as soon as we make them. Other decisions last years and years beyond the moment of deciding. They ripple like waves through history, affecting time far beyond that first instant. Even the smallest of decisions has potential to shape us at our core. A slight waver, an easy "yes" over "no" can literally change a person's life.

Certain choices carry more possibilities for the ripple effect than others do. Decisions regarding morality and sexual purity are much more complicated than "Should I have the cheeseburger or the chicken fingers?" and "Would I like fries with that?" A greasy lunch might give you momentary heartburn and happiness, but it won't affect you much beyond that. The decision to lie, on the other hand, could affect a person for years after the fact. So could the decision to steal, the decision to cheat, the decision to have sex outside of marriage. With these last few choices, ripples grow from small and seemingly trivial to very large and very considerable. As months and years pass, ripples get bigger, their emotional effects dig in deeper, and their hold on us gets stronger and more fierce.

God gives people guidelines—not to keep us from enjoying life, but to keep us from having to ride the waves of poor choices. He is not in the habit of withholding things out of spite. He simply wants to offer us the best life possible: a life with as few ripples as possible. How many ripples are you creating for yourself?

—Lisa Velthouse

 FAQ

Q. Are the consequences of sexual sin really that bad?
A. More than most people realize.

Flee from sexual immorality. All other sins a man commits are outside his body, but he who sins sexually sins against his own body. (1 Corinthians 6:18)

Through this verse we can see that God has a full awareness and understanding of the effects of sexual sin in our lives. Our sexual thoughts, images, and experiences become part of our memories. These thoughts, images, and experiences stay with us forever. Keeping a clean heart and mind, and avoiding this area of sin—with the ever-present help of the Holy Spirit—is the best way to eliminate the negative effects of sexual sin.

Q. My boyfriend and I have not "gone all the way," but does the Bible say anything about just getting physical without having sex?
A. Yes: Refrain and flee! Your honor and purity are at stake when you become involved in lustful passions.

It is God's will that you should be sanctified: that you should avoid sexual immorality; that each of you should learn to control his own body in a way that is holy and honorable, not in passionate lust like the heathen, who do not know God.
(1 Thessalonians 4:3–5)

Each time that we "get physical," we break down the walls of resistance a little more. Although we convince ourselves that we can control these feelings and emotions, it is difficult to control our emotions and physical self in the midst of the experience. The best strategy is avoidance.

Q. What is the difference between lusting and looking?
A. Sin. Lusting occurs when you welcome a temptation, concentrate your whole mind on it, or fantasize about it.

You have heard that it was said, "Do not commit adultery." But I tell you that anyone who looks at a woman lustfully has already committed adultery with her in her heart. (Matthew 5:27–28)

That first look is often a normal reaction. It is that second sustained look that is the beginning of lust, the point where the thoughts of our mind take over the process.

Q. If a denomination approves of homosexuality, and even confirms a gay bishop, shouldn't we take another look at this issue?

A. The Bible is straightforward about homosexuality being a sin. If you take a second look at the issue, do so by reading Scriptures on the subject. The most-often quoted verses are from Romans 1, in which homosexual behavior, whether between two women or two men, is harshly condemned. It's not only referred to as wrong, but as a manifestation of evil. Next, go to your Bible's index and seek out other Scriptures that do the same, in both the Old and New Testaments. A pastor is to be above reproach in all that he or she does, so it makes little sense to defend this issue unless you're willing to ignore the Bible's teaching. See this chapter's introduction for a deeper treatment of this question.

 # Reaction and Reflection

In this chapter, we have discussed some issues close to the core of who we are as people facing the daily challenges of living according to God's commands. Please consider the following questions as they relate to your individual walk with Christ.

1. What are your greatest obstacles to living a morally and sexually pure life?

2. What areas of temptation contribute to these obstacles?

3. What is your plan to keep or begin practicing moral and sexual purity?

4. Are there people in your life who can serve as sources of accountability? Who are they?

5. What is the status of your pursuit for a closer relationship with God?
    *   How much time per week are you spending in God's Word?

    *   How often are you communicating with God through prayer?

    *   Are you spending time with other believers in worship and fellowship? How often and in what ways?

6. Are you currently involved in a dating relationship?

   • Is this individual a believer in Jesus Christ?

   • What are some evidences that God is part of your relationship?

7. What are some challenges that you face in this relationship in regard to sexual purity?

   • How might you initiate a conversation in these areas?

Suggested Readings and Resources

Cloud, H., and John Townsend. *Boundaries in Dating*. Grand Rapids, MI: Zondervan, 2000.

Harris, J. *I Kissed Dating Goodbye: A New Attitude Toward Relationships and Romance*. Portland, OR: Multnomah, 1997.

Kidder, R. M. *How Good People Make Tough Choices*. New York: William Morrow and Company, 1995.

Laurie, G. *God's Design for Christian Marriages.* Eugene, OR: Harvest House Publishers, 1983.

McDonald, G. *When Men Think Private Thoughts.* Nashville: Thomas Nelson Publishers, 1996.

Peters, C. *Navigating Toward Home.* Mobile, AL: Evergreen Press, 2000.

Roberts, T. and Jack Hayford. *Pure Desire: Helping People Break Free From Sexual Struggles.* Ventura, CA: Regal Books, 1999.

St. Clair, B., and Bill Jones. *Dating: Picking (and Being) a Winner.* San Bernadino, CA: Here's Life Publishers, 1987.

Sherman, D., and William Hendricks. *Keeping Your Ethical Edge Sharp.* Colorado Springs: Navpress, 1990.

Endnotes

1. Jerry Pattengale, *Chronicle-Tribune*, September 25, 2003.

2. Sexuality Information and Education Council of the United States (SIECUS), press release, January 18, 2000. Available online at www.siecus.org/media/press/press007.html (accessed August 7, 2007).

3. http://www.occoc.com/character/What_is_Character.pdf (accessed August 7, 2007).

4. Thomas Lickona, *Educating for Character* (New York: Bantam Books, 1991).

5. Craig Peters, *Navigating Toward Home: Charting Your Course Toward Biblical Manhood* (Mobile, AL: Evergreen Press, 2000), 90-91.

6. Parents Television Council, press release, November 8, 1997. Available online at www.parents.org/ptc/publications/reports.archives/famhtm.asp (accessed August 7, 2007).

7. The Barna Group. http://www.barna.org (accessed August 5, 2007).

8. Rushworth Kidder, *How Good People Make Tough Choices: Resolving the Dilemmas of Ethical Living* (New York: Fireside Publishers, 1996).

9. Joshua Harris, *I Kissed Dating Goodbye: A New Attitude Toward Relationships and Romance* (Portland, OR: Multnomah Publishers, 1997).

10. Charlie Riggs, *Learning to Walk With God* (Charlotte, NC: Grason, 1989).

11. Barry St. Clair and Bill Jones, *Dating: Picking and Being a Winner* (San Bernadino, CA: Here's Life Publishers, 1987).

5

faith
in action

serving Christ through vocation

*Therefore, I urge you, brothers, in view of God's mercy,
to offer your bodies as living sacrifices, holy and pleasing to
God—this is your spiritual act of worship. Do not conform any
longer to the pattern of this world, but be transformed by the
renewing of your mind. Then you will be able to test and approve
what God's will is—his good, pleasing and perfect will.*
(Romans 12:1–2)

a church's memory:
george the janitor

At 19 years of age, in a monastic gift shop on an Israeli hillside, I met the sweetest yet homeliest woman I've ever seen. She was a frail wrinkled nun working the counter—the main greeter for her nunnery. I looked up to hand her my money and was shocked into hesitation. Hundreds of grotesque warts covered the entire left side of her face, chin, most of her nose, and what showed of her forehead. Big cauliflower warts. Small pinhead dark warts. Long warts. Short warts. She had them all.

At first I wanted to ask her about them. After all, I was young and curious, she was saintly and kind. But her siren voice and inviting smile won over my curiosity, and we began to talk about her decision to become a nun. She was excited and yet humble about such an important role—serving God in "His holy land." There was an inner peace and a joyous spirit that any sensible human would crave. Her gifts, her looks, her smile, and her insightfulness all seemed perfect for that position—one she had held for decades. And, very likely, it was a perfect fit—God had orchestrated it.

As a public speaker and professor, I'm regularly impressed with individuals, like that sister, who are content and fulfilled in out-of-the-way places. I've often thought of another such individual, George. He was the janitor for his modest country church in the deep South. Let me give you a glimpse of his contentment with his job, and his focus on his church's needs.

His backward community lacked musicians and relied on a distant college for mercenary pianists, when one could be found. The story picks up at a lively time in that little church's worship history. For the previous two years, the vibrant little body of believers had been blessed with piano music—beautiful melodies. The music made one want to dance, though nobody did. The saints smiled a lot in those days. Oh, maybe not during announcements, but when the music began, when the air filled with the great hymns, the individual moods always melted into one of harmony. Visitors were even spotted on occasion.

These had been two joyful years, but they were about to end. The lively young pianist was about to graduate and no other musician could be found. Nobody was more saddened by the prospective silence than the janitor, though he never shared his feelings. Always private. Always.

Rev. Steve Wright noticed that George had been at the church late on numerous occasions. One night, quite by accident, he stopped when he noticed George's lone car in the parking lot. The pastor eased into the church only to be confronted by dissonant sounds coming from the keyboard. Awkward arrangements. Unrecognizable. And the biggest shock was that George was producing them, hunched over a practice book. The lead-fingered recluse, startled by his unannounced audience, immediately and repeatedly apologized for his actions. He said he would never play again. Pastor Wright calmed him and asked why he had decided to take up piano late in life. George attempted an explanation in spite of his red cheeks and cowering posture: "Rev. Wright, I just thought that . . . well . . . you see . . ."

After much stammering and Rev. Wright's coaching, George the janitor explained that the piano music had been a tremendous blessing to the congregation. The thought of not having it so saddened him that maybe, with God's help, just maybe, he could learn at least a couple of songs to play—in the event that no pianist was located by year's end. As you can imagine, my friend Steve was moved. He encouraged George to continue, although George remained embarrassed about the incident. The months passed without any more audiences, though his car occasionally was spotted at the church late.

The Sunday came when no pianist sat at the keyboard. Unannounced, George slipped from his seat to the bench. Snickers, astonishment, disbelief. Well, you can imagine the reaction from his friends who had known him from a distance for decades. But when he began stumbling through some choruses, recognizable but unpolished, his friends knew that this was serious. George just wanted to help them to worship. By the third elementary song, every last member was singing with unbridled passion and emotion, from the heart and from the soul. They understood George's sacrifice and selflessness. As George finished and moved toward what had been his hiding place for years—the very end of the pew—the teary-eyed congregation responded in one accord to give him a standing ovation. George did not seek recognition. He probably thought the applause was for God.

Some members still say the best music that ever graced their little church was during those few Sundays that George the janitor played.

George served the Lord as a janitor. That was his vocation, his job. I can only assume from my friend's comments that George was content; in fact, he loved his work. Although he wasn't a pastor or in "full-time" ministry, his life was focused on serving and honoring God.

Other people, like the nun in Israel, are at peace in their ministries and would likely be frustrated otherwise. This chapter looks at the important issue of finding the right vocation.

faith
in action

serving Christ through vocation

 ## Consider the Source

The LORD God took the man and put him in the Garden of Eden to work it and take care of it. (Genesis 2:15)

Understand the Need

After creating Adam, God placed him in the Garden of Eden. As described above, Adam was given specific responsibilities regarding the care and maintenance of the garden. Additionally, God gave Adam the task of naming all of the animals on the earth (Genesis 2:19–20). From the beginning it was apparent that God not only created man and woman as inhabitants of the earth, but He also created them for specific tasks. After Adam and Eve were removed from the garden as a result of their sin against God, the concept of work took on a different and more challenging meaning:

> *To Adam he said, "Because you listened to your wife and ate from the tree about which I commanded you, 'You must not eat of it,'*

"Cursed is the ground because of you; through painful toil you will eat of it all the days of your life . . . By the sweat of your brow you will eat your food . . ." (Genesis 3:17, 19)

In today's world, work continues to be a critical part of our existence. We spend a major portion of our waking hours engaged in work. According to Doug Sherman and William Hendricks, work has been secularized and the world has created a high premium on the meaning and value of work in our lives:

- The secular view of work expects more of work and self than work and self can deliver.
- The secular view of work tends to make an idol of career.
- The secular view of work leaves God out of its system.[1]

As Christians, it is important to evaluate the role of work in our lives as it relates to God's Word and the pursuit of His will. Christians are to serve God faithfully in every situation, including their places of employment. Although the vast majority of Christians are not in "Christian" vocations, the example we set in the workplace is a strong and influential witness to others. If you are a Christian, is this true for you? And remember, the need to spread the gospel involves more than simply preaching and teaching:

Just as each of us has one body with many members, and these members do not all have the same function, so in Christ we who are many form one body, and each member belongs to all the others. We have different gifts, according to the grace given us. If a man's gift is prophesying, let him use it in proportion to his faith. If it is serving, let him serve; if it is teaching, let him teach; if it is encouraging, let him encourage; if it is contributing to the needs of others, let him give generously; if it is leadership, let him govern diligently; if it is showing mercy, let him do it cheerfully. (Romans 12:4–8)

Consider the following argument for thinking about your place of employment as a valuable location for serving the Lord and communicating the gospel message:

Suppose you and I decided that we wanted to hold a week-long evangelistic crusade in your city. We'd have to start months ahead of time to plan it, to line up our helpers, and to raise the money. After considerable effort and expense by scores of people, we might be able to attract a total attendance of 5,000, maybe as many as 10,000 or 20,000 if we had a well-known evangelist speak. That would be a one-time event. And we'd hope that we would see a few hundred people come to faith in Christ.

Now by contrast, think about your workplace. Every day your employer brings together dozens if not hundreds of workers. He pays for the building, and he gives you eight hours a day to be with them—day after day. Furthermore, there are quite likely others around you who also have a relationship with Christ. Collectively, you have an impressive opportunity for influence . . .

How long will it be before Christians wake up to this reality? Most of us think of "ministry" and religious activity as something we do on our own time. Activities like Bible studies, volunteer projects, prayer meetings, softball games, pool parties, concerts—these are where we put our time and energy on behalf of our "Christian life." But like a set of golf clubs or the lawn mower, we put our religion away when it's time to go back to work, to the "real world."[2]

Christian Vocations

Throughout the Bible are examples of individuals whose vocations concentrate on the needs of God's followers, or on sharing and/or defending the

> It is not what a man does that determines whether his work is sacred or secular, it is why he does it. The motive is everything.
>
> A.W. Tozer
> *The Pursuit of God*[3]

biblical doctrines (apologetics). Christians often refer to these ministry-oriented vocations as "full-time Christian service." The Christian vocation is identified today with such occupations as pastor, priest, preacher, missionary, teacher at a Christian school, evangelist, and music minister, to name a few. In principle, similar types of jobs (callings or ministries) existed among the Old Testament Jews, who were known as "Hebrews" or "Israelites," and among the early Christians.

So now, go. I am sending you [Moses] to Pharaoh to bring my people the Israelites out of Egypt. (Exodus 3:10)

Appoint the Levites [an Israelite clan] to be in charge of the tabernacle of the Testimony—over all its furnishings and everything belonging to it. They are to carry the tabernacle and all its furnishings; they are to take care of it and encamp around it. (Numbers 1:50)

So the Twelve gathered all the disciples together and said, "It would not be right for us to neglect the ministry of the word of God in order to wait on tables." (Acts 6:2)

The Call

Playing to Our Strengths

God has given each of us a unique set of skills, talents, and abilities, not unlike a treasure box full of amazing things that we must explore and figure out how to enjoy. He has promised us in His Word that He has a plan for each of us, "plans to prosper you and not to harm you, plans to give you hope and a future" (Jeremiah 29:11). So, why would He give us special skills if they weren't part of His plan? The trick is for us to learn to play to our strengths. That is, the skills God gave us. Will that automatically win people to Christ? No, but if we remember to "do it all for the glory of God" and do our best to be imitators of Christ, we can be assured others will take notice.

—Mike Cline

The word "vocation" comes from the Latin verb vocare, "to call." There are those who believe that God gives a distinct call to believers even today and that those planning on careers in full-time Christian service ought to have a sense of God's calling on their lives. Arguments also can be made to the effect that God uses people in all walks of life:

> In other words, you can go to church and pray (a "sacred" category) and still be in sin. You may recite a creed or partake of the elements yet retain hateful thoughts toward someone who has wronged you. Or sit there and dream about your ambitions, and how fulfilling them will give you esteem, power, or money. Or skip on the offering because some church leader has said something that offended you.
>
> On the other hand, you can go to work in an office where the atmosphere is very "secular"—the conversation is littered with profanity, the jokes are off-color, the work is often slipshod, the politics are wearisome. And yet, like Daniel or Joseph in the Old Testament, you can keep your conversation pure and your behavior above reproach. You can do your work with integrity even if others do not. You can honor and obey God in a very worldly environment.
>
> In short, God's interest is not simply that we participate in holy activities but that we become holy. Not pious. Not sanctimonious. Not worldly. But pure, healthy, Christlike.[4]

For some, the call comes as a dramatic event that has a mystical aspect. This call would be similar to that which the prophet Isaiah received:

> *In the year that King Uzziah died, I saw the Lord seated on a throne, high and exalted . . . Then I heard the voice of the Lord saying, "Whom shall I send? And who will go for us?" And I said, "Here am I. Send me!"* (Isaiah 6:1, 8)

or the Apostle Paul:

About noon as I came near Damascus, suddenly a bright light from heaven flashed around me. I fell to the ground and heard a voice say to me, "Saul, Saul!" [Paul's name before his conversion.] (Acts 22:6–7)

Although we are often led to believe that great Christian leaders have received dramatic calls of this type, we are more likely to experience a gradual inner sense of God's leading that grows in strength and clarity over time. In any case, whether dramatic or subtle, the true test of a divine calling (vocation) upon one's life is a deep unshakable conviction that God has directed a person toward a particular ministry, whether full-time and church-related or otherwise:

Yet when I preach the gospel, I cannot boast, for I am compelled to preach. Woe to me if I do not preach the gospel! (1 Corinthians 9:16)

When God calls a person into special service, He will send that individual with His power and authority. The key issue is not whether you will be a Christian in a secular workplace or one in a Christian vocation—the key is self-surrender:

But seek first his kingdom and his righteousness, and all these things will be given to you as well. (Matthew 6:33)

But the Lord said to Ananias, "Go! This man is my chosen instrument to carry my name before the Gentiles and their kings and before the people of Israel." (Acts 9:15)

Therefore, I urge you, brothers, in view of God's mercy, to offer your bodies as living sacrifices, holy and pleasing to God—this is your spiritual act of worship. Do not conform any longer to the pattern of this world, but be transformed by the renewing of your mind. Then you will be able to test and approve what God's will is—his good, pleasing and perfect will. (Romans 12:1–2)

God's Guidance

A Call to Jail

As a former police officer I was nervous when I felt led to become a jail chaplain. Would inmates accept me? Why would God call someone to serve as a chaplain without any formal ministerial training? I think it was because I finally decided to obey completely and follow Him. Because of that decision I have been blessed beyond measure. Is God calling you outside of your comfort zone?

—Jack Brady

Becoming a Christian involves trusting God with all of the details of your life. Your faith is ever important. God has a purpose for you, a plan for your life. The power of the Holy Spirit will be with you. You may find yourself in many unique situations, but you will not be alone.

The Spirit clearly says that in later times some will abandon the faith and follow deceiving spirits and things taught by demons. Such teachings come through hypocritical liars, whose consciences have been seared as with a hot iron. They forbid people to marry and order them to abstain from certain foods, which God created to be received with thanksgiving by those who believe and who know the truth. For everything God created is good, and nothing is to be rejected if it is received with thanksgiving, because it is consecrated by the word of God and prayer.

If you point these things out to the brothers, you will be a good minister of Christ Jesus, brought up in the truths of the faith and of the good teaching that you have followed. Have nothing to do with godless myths and old wives' tales; rather, train yourself to be godly. For physical training is of some value, but godliness has value for all things, holding promise for both the present life and the life to come.

This is a trustworthy saying that deserves full acceptance (and for this we labor and strive), that we have put our hope in the living God, who is the Savior of all men, and especially of those who believe.

Command and teach these things. Don't let anyone look down on you because you are young, but set an example for the believers in speech, in life, in love, in faith and in purity. Until I come, devote yourself to the public reading of Scripture, to preaching and to teaching. Do not neglect your gift, which was given you through a prophetic message when the body of elders laid their hands on you.

Be diligent in these matters; give yourself wholly to them, so that everyone may see your progress. Watch your life and doctrine closely. Persevere in them, because if you do, you will save both yourself and your hearers. (1 Timothy 4)

He has made us competent as ministers of a new covenant— not of the letter but of the Spirit; for the letter kills, but the Spirit gives life. (2 Corinthians 3:6)

There are different kinds of gifts, but the same Spirit. (1 Corinthians 12:4)

All these are the work of one and the same Spirit, and he gives them to each one, just as he determines. (1 Corinthians 12:11)

> **Understanding the Pressure**
>
> Have you ever hammered chocolate chips into a sugar cookie trying to make it into a chocolate chip cookie? In the end you fail and destroy a perfectly good cookie as well. During most of my years in elementary and high school, those around me tried to force me to become what I was never designed to be. That didn't work either. Your vocation should be based on who you are and the unique purpose this gives you, and then find the place you can fulfill this.
>
> —Bill Millard

There is incredible diversity in the gifts that God gives us and in the way He calls us to use those gifts. We must never assume that God's guidance will short-circuit our ability to reason for ourselves and to be creative in following His ways. We can be assured that if we maintain a close personal relationship with God, He will communicate His desires for our lives.

God's Promises

We know from the Old Testament that God's promises (except those related to salvation) are for believers only:

Blessed is he
whose transgressions are forgiven,
whose sins are covered.
Blessed is the man
whose sin the LORD does not count against him
and in whose spirit is no deceit.
When I kept silent,
my bones wasted away
through my groaning all day long.
For day and night
your hand was heavy upon me;
my strength was sapped
as in the heat of summer. (Selah)
Then I acknowledged my sin to you

and did not cover up my iniquity.
I said, "I will confess
my transgressions to the LORD"—
and you forgave
the guilt of my sin. (Selah)
Therefore let everyone who is godly pray to you
while you may be found;
surely when the mighty waters rise,
they will not reach him.
You are my hiding place;
you will protect me from trouble
and surround me with songs of deliverance. (Selah)
I will instruct you and teach you in the way you should go;
I will counsel you and watch over you.
Do not be like the horse or the mule,
which have no understanding
but must be controlled by bit and bridle
or they will not come to you.
Many are the woes of the wicked,
but the LORD's unfailing love
surrounds the man who trusts in him.
Rejoice in the LORD and be glad, you righteous;
sing, all you who are upright in heart! (Psalm 32)

What promises are you claiming? Consider the following:

And you also were included in Christ when you heard the word of truth, the gospel of your salvation. Having believed, you were marked in him with a seal, the promised Holy Spirit. (Ephesians 1:13)

Working with Excellence

Whatever you do, work at it with all your heart, as working for the Lord, not for men. (Colossians 3:23)

We are all familiar with numerous situations in which individuals have chosen to engage in unscrupulous or shoddy work practices.

White-collar crimes, insider stock trading, calling in sick to get a day off work, stealing office products, or simply not giving a day's work for a day's pay are examples of employees treating their work life with limited levels of integrity. Some of these seem to be inconsequential, especially when compared to large-scale scandals such as Enron that have resulted in the loss of millions of dollars and numerous jobs. However, as Christians, we are

Nine Workplace Attitudes Bosses Hate[5]	
NMJ:	Not My Job
NMM:	Need More Money
WCT:	Wastes Company Time
PPP:	Promises, Promises, Promises
NMH:	Needs More Help
ACD:	Always Complaining and Disagreeable
CWS:	Clock Watcher's Syndrome
TTM:	The Trouble Maker
SRM:	Supports Rumor Mill

expected to meet a higher standard than that of others in the workplace. We are called to live and work according to God's standards of behavior.

If we plan to take seriously the responsibility of treating our workplace as a location for sharing the gospel message, then we also must consider the testimony presented by our work ethics and interactions. As Jesus commanded us, we are to be "salt" and "light" in the world (Matthew 5:13, 14). The things we do, the comments we make, and the level of integrity that we demonstrate in the workplace should present a positive image of Christ to those with whom we work.

You may find yourself in a job with an employer or a location that you do not view as ideal. In that circumstance, you may ask yourself, "Why did God put me here?" or "I can't believe that this is what God wants me to be doing with my life." Your perception and image of an ideal job may not match where God has you serving. On the other hand, your positive attitude, willingness to work hard, and commitment to doing the right thing may be the best possible testimony to non-Christians around you—better than any sermon they could hear. Be salt and light!

A Final Thought on Vocation and Calling

As a means of summarizing our discussion, consider the following observations on vocation, life calling, and world-changing endeavors:

For the sake of argument, let me assume that you have a career. There is something for which you see yourself best suited to make a living. You expect that career to make it possible for you to pay your bills, take care of your family responsibilities, and provide a certain standard of living. You probably also expect it to provide certain less-tangible rewards as titles and social standing.

But do you also have a calling? Consistent with the way most people hear that term, a calling involves a clear sense of being commissioned by God for some task. It is your pursuit of the sovereignty of God over who you are and what you are doing with your life. It is the sense that God's hand is on you and that he has a sense of genuine pleasure in what you are doing.

The real secret to fulfillment in one's life is to have career and calling merged into one. Don't you suspect Billy Graham views his as one and the same? But what about you?

I believe God has given you an opportunity to make a difference in the world. I am convinced he wants you to change the world. And I further believe that he wants you to see your job, business, or profession as an extension of the kingdom of heaven. Here's what I mean by all this.

The sense that one's career is also a holy calling shouldn't startle us. If slaves-become-Christians were counseled to *"render service with enthusiasm, as to the Lord and not to men and women, knowing that whatever good we do, we will receive the same again from the Lord"* (Ephesians 6:7–8), then surely you are supposed to be the best employee or employer the Acme Widget Company has ever seen. If not, why not?

Above paycheck or promotion, do something that contributes to the good of your world. Let your routine tasks reflect the character and excellence heaven is building into your life. Understand that your work is inseparable from your spiritual life—and reflects its authenticity. When your faith cleanses and consecrates your workplace to God, you have found a calling larger than your career.

Solomon put it this way: *"There is nothing better for mortals than to eat and drink, and find enjoyment in their work. This, I saw, is from the hand of God; for apart from him who can eat or who can have enjoyment?"* (Ecclesiastes 2:24–25)

How will you change the world today? God is ready to be your partner.[6]

On Becoming

I can still hear the dinner bell tolling, smell the aroma of fried chicken wafting its way from the dining hall, and feel the tenseness of my tiny tummy as I kneeled on the cold concrete floor of the campground children's chapel. It was noon, certainly time for a hungry five-year-old boy to eat some lunch. But something more important captured my attention. At the close of the Bible lesson, we were invited to pray at the altar. Without hesitation I responded to the invitation chorus, *"Into my heart, into my heart; come into my heart, Lord Jesus. Come in today; come in to stay. Come into my heart, Lord Jesus."*[7]

Why would I, a kid who had grown up in a Christian home, need to exchange lunch for leaning over a wooden bench to talk to a God I couldn't see? Perhaps it was due in part to the emotion I sensed – the children's minister was urging us to "seek the Lord while He may be found," while vividly portraying the consequences of failing that pursuit. But more realistically, I think it was due to God's Holy Spirit causing me to sense my *heart condition.* Even at five years old I recognized right from wrong, knowing I was a sinner who needed to make a 180-degree turn. Most certainly, I did not know the theological implications of *sinner* nor did I have a very long list of sins to confess. I just knew my heart was dirty, and the only way to get it cleaned up was to talk to God about it.

Several dramatic changes resulted immediately — the nasty words, disobedience to my parents, and ugly, hateful attitudes stopped. I had become a new person from the inside out. And, now as I review the following years, I realize the importance of the continual cleansing of Christ's blood. His daily presence in my life that began on that hot August afternoon is still with me. What a fantastic way to live!

FAQ

Q. What about the role of a girlfriend/boyfriend in this new calling to Christian service?

A. His or her role depends first on an individual commitment to Christ. Secondly, it depends on your commitment to Christ, the giver of eternal life. If He has arranged the cosmos, and has control of the world's future and your eternal destination, He also can direct you in this matter. If you rely on Him, God will provide the special partner to work with you, if and when you are to marry. Balance that person's advice with that of other Christian couples from similar organizations and your ongoing consultation with the Scriptures and responses to prayer.

Q. Does God call those who are not planning on "full-time Christian service?"

A. All believers receive a call from God to obey His commandments (John 14:15), share the gospel with others (Acts 1:8), and follow Christ (Luke 9:23). Those entering full-time Christian service should expect to receive a divine command to commit to a life of service in the kingdom of God. Sometimes, individuals sense a specific leading in their lives to enter other more secularly oriented vocations such as nursing, business, or teaching. Others do not. Both can legitimately feel they are serving God with their life-calling, whether or not they are "divinely called." In either case, surrender of one's life to the will of God is the primary concern.

 Reaction and Reflection

An important aspect of your career as a university student is preparation for some type of vocation and career. You have chosen a major based on your current expectations for future employment and service.

1. How and why did you choose to engage in your current course of study?

2. What evidence do you have that God has led you in this direction?

3. How do you view the connection between what you have chosen to do for a career and the idea of "full-time Christian service?"

4. How might you effectively serve as a witness for Jesus Christ in your chosen field? Provide some examples or scenarios.

The Call of a Lifetime

Keith Drury has influenced hundreds of pastors and lay leaders over the past four decades, including the primary author of this text. Keith continues to do so through his recent book, *The Call of a Lifetime*.[8] This book is written for the person "called" or trying to determine a "call" to a full-time profession in Christian ministry. The following excerpts will afford you a glimpse of his helpful insights:

. . . the *call* is God's recruitment of Christians into the ministry as a lifelong profession (p. 30)

. . . the call to *the* ministry is an inner conviction that God wants me to serve Him for life as a professional minister (p. 36)

. . . while it is true that God calls everyone to minister to others, God does not call everyone into professional ministry as a lifetime vocation (p. 38)

. . . if God has called you to the ministry, then He has called you to take the time and effort to prepare for life in this vocation (p. 122)

Suggested Readings and Resources

Books

Addington, T. G., and Stephen R. Graves. *Building Blocks for Your Life@Work.* Nashville: W Publishing Group/Thomas Nelson, 2000.

Blackaby, H. T., and Kerry L. Skinner. *Called and Accountable.* Birmingham, AL: New Hope Publishers, 2002.

Drury, K. *The Call of a Lifetime.* Indianapolis: Wesleyan Publishing House, 2003.

Guinness, O. *The Call.* Nashville: Word Publishing, 1998.

Graves, S. R., and T. G. Addington. *Behind the Bottom Line: Powering Business Life with Spiritual Wisdom.* Nashville: W Publishing Group/Thomas Nelson, 2002.

Julian, L. S. *God is My CEO.* Avon, MA: Adams Media Corporation, 2001.

Maxwell, J. *Becoming a Person of Influence.* Nashville: Thomas Nelson, 1997.

———. *Your Road Map to Success.* Nashville: Thomas Nelson, 2002.

MacDonald, G. *Ordering Your Private World.* Rev. ed. Nashville: Thomas Nelson, 2002.

Palmer, P. *Let Your Life Speak: Listening for the Voice of Vocation.* New York: Jossey-Bass, 1999.

Sherman, D., and William Hendricks. *Your Work Matters to God.* Colorado Springs: Navpress, 1987.

Other Resources

Center for Life Calling and Leadership. http://www.clcl.indwes.edu

Endnotes

1. Doug Sherman and William Hendricks, *Your Work Matters to God* (Colorado Springs: Navpress, 1987), 33-39.

2. Ibid.

3. A. W. Tozer, *The Pursuit of God* (Camp Hill, PA: Christian Publications, Inc., 1982), first published in 1948.

4. Sherman and Hendricks, *Your Work Matters to God*, 54-55.

5. "Nine Workplace Attitudes Bosses Hate," in *Connected through Relationships to Those in Authority* at http://www.bc.irvingbible.org/resources/ln_authority.doc (accessed August 7, 2007).

6. Rubel Shelly, "Your Chance to Change the World," found at Faithful Hope Reading Room. Available online at http://www.faithfulhope.com/readingroom (accessed August 7, 2007).

7. Clarke, Harry D., *Into My Heart"* (Carol Stream, IL: Hope Publishing Company, 1952).

8. Keith Drury, *The Call of a Lifetime* (Indianapolis: Wesleyan Publishing House, 2003).

6

introducing Christ

the mandate of evangelism

All authority in heaven and on earth has been given to me. Therefore go and make disciples of all nations, baptizing them in the name of the Father and of the Son and of the Holy Spirit, and teaching them to obey everything I have commanded you. And surely I am with you always, to the very end of the age.
(Matthew 28:18–20)

an NBA memory:
learning which doors to open

I jumped into Oscar Robinson's car and asked him the all-important question: "Have you heard the good news?" The basketball icon tolerated my rude and uninvited entrance to his Z-28, removed his ecru western hat, and politely responded, "Well, young man, I'm not sure," and he paused with a friendly glimmer in his eye, "but I assume you're about to tell me." He smiled gracefully, and motioned for me to continue.

At seventeen years of age, and as a new Christian, about all I knew to do was to share the gospel message. So, with the best of intentions, I did.

"Mr. Robinson," I continued, "if you believe in the Bible and Jesus Christ, you'll go to heaven. If you don't, you won't."

He waited for a pause, and then seemed to thank me sincerely. His kindness overwhelmed me. I recall shaking his big hand, noticing his left knee's tight fit in that sports car, and thanking him for his time. I returned to my job at the Holiday Inn desk, assuming by his actions and response that he was already a Christian—and, for the first time, considering that perhaps my approach to evangelism was not the best.

At the end of that spring break I returned to my classes, which included the unique course, "Church Growth and Evangelism." Although I ended up doing graduate and doctoral work in psychology and ancient history, this course helped me to understand my new faith—and it remains a positive college memory. At the end of one of the lectures on evangelism, the stately professor asked if there were any questions.

"Sir," I asked with loud naïveté, "will you share a story with us about a recent time you shared the plan of salvation?" I assumed that the motivating lecturer would have plenty of illustrations, perhaps as recent as that week. This was a class on evangelism, and as we said back then, "That dog could hunt." He was smooth. Funny. Creative. Energetic.

Class became instantly awkward . . . my question, though innocent, became embarrassing. A few disjointed cotton-mouthed sentences followed. Rambling. Yada yada yada. He eventually answered, admitting it had been a while since he had witnessed, and then he shared a story from his early years in the ministry.

This reflection on evangelism convicts me—now a middle-aged professor. Do I look at evangelism with the same enthusiasm and commitment as in my earlier years? If evangelism includes only the asking of direct personal questions, probably not.

Should the same question I asked my professor come from one of my students, how would I answer? Well, I haven't jumped into anyone's car lately. Nor do I have any recent stories about interrupting beach couples with my *Four Spiritual Laws*.

I share my faith, but usually in indirect ways and to many types of people. Whether it's through a values-based presentation to a national audience on education, a recent article in the *Chicago Tribune* on life purpose, or a friendly discussion on a cross-country flight that becomes serious, I'm conscious about representing the biblical message. But do I run regularly to people to witness? No.

There comes a time, regardless of context or setting, in which people need to hear, read, or see the clear plan of salvation in order to make a personal decision. This is what is most commonly referred to as evangelism. As this chapter points out, it's helpful to be clear in the presentation. To do so requires a clear understanding. Also, unlike my college question and actions, you will find in this chapter that evangelism is also much more than boldness and energy. It's a lifestyle.

introducing Christ

the mandate of evangelism

 ## Consider the Source

J esus clearly instructs His followers to share the gospel (i.e., the good news of His life and Resurrection). The following passage was a central part of His instructions to the disciples in anticipation and preparation for His impending departure from them:

All authority in heaven and on earth has been given to me. Therefore go and make disciples of all nations, baptizing them in the name of the Father and of the Son and of the Holy Spirit, and teaching them to obey everything I have commanded you. And surely I am with you always, to the very end of the age. (Matthew 28:18–20)

The recorded words of Christ are clear—believers are commanded to share their faith. The purpose of sharing, as defined by Jesus, is to explain the plan of salvation in order that the listener or reader might believe, have eternal life, and devote his or her life to obediently following Him as a disciple.

This chapter will provide you with a glimpse of the scriptural mandate for "Christian evangelism" and focus on the "why" of evangelism. In chapter 7 you will learn some basic strategies for sharing your faith with others through witnessing.

Understand the Need

How, then, can they call on the one they have not believed in? And how can they believe in the one of whom they have not heard? And how can they hear without someone preaching to them? (Romans 10:14)

Paul's questions represent the challenge of evangelism. It takes a "preacher"—someone who can clearly proclaim the message of Christ—to present the gospel. With the radical advances in technology since the first century, this same message may be proclaimed by a "preacher" who is adept at communicating accurately in a medium other than speaking (e.g., written word, video, DVD, Internet, music). The message, which has never changed, is the most important thing, and a good messenger will relay it clearly, just as Paul does in the following passage:

Just as man is destined to die once, and after that to face judgment, so Christ was sacrificed once to take away the sins of many people; and he will appear a second time, not to bear sin, but to bring salvation to those who are waiting for him. (Hebrews 9:27–28)

All people will eventually face the end of life here on earth, either through death or the "second coming" of Jesus Christ. He proclaimed that He is returning to earth. Only those who are ready, the "born again," will participate in the new order of reality He will establish here on earth:

For the Lord himself will come down from heaven, with a loud command, with the voice of the archangel and with the trumpet call of God, and the dead in Christ will rise first. After that, we who are still alive and are left will be caught up together with them in the clouds to meet the Lord in the air. And so we will be with the Lord forever. Therefore encourage each other with these words. (1 Thessalonians 4:16–18)

Do these words encourage you and bring you hope? This is a comforting thought for the Christian. For non-Christians, however, there is no hope of sharing God's coming triumph, either when Christ returns or at the time of their deaths. So, what about your friends and relatives? Although you are not held accountable for their actions and responses, you are responsible for presenting Christ to them. This occurs through the evidence of your words, actions, lifestyle, and, as the Spirit leads you, through direct presentations of the gospel:

"My food," said Jesus, *"is to do the will of him who sent me and to finish his work. Do you not say, 'Four months more and then the harvest'? I tell you, open your eyes and look at the fields! They are ripe for harvest. Even now the reaper draws his wages, even now he harvests the crop for eternal life, so that the sower and the reaper may be glad together. Thus the saying 'One sows and another reaps' is true. I sent you to reap what you have not worked for. Others have done the hard work, and you have reaped the benefits of their labor."* (John 4:34–38)

Lessons from Jesus and His Original Disciples

The best place to get a sense of evangelism is to examine the relationship between Jesus, His disciples, and their external world. Jesus called His disciples and commissioned them for service:

He appointed twelve—designating them apostles—that they might be with him and that he might send them out to preach and to have authority to drive out demons (Mark 3:14–15; see also John 20:21).

These chosen individuals would be His traveling companions, the focus of His energy, the beneficiaries of His teaching, the means by which the Word would be spread after His departure, and the future foundations of His church. The process was perfect and the results were phenomenal.

After a brief period of orientation and training, Jesus told the disciples that they were going on a road trip:

> *Calling the Twelve to him, he sent them out two by two and gave them authority over evil spirits.*
>
> *These were his instructions: "Take nothing for the journey except a staff—no bread, no bag, no money in your belts. Wear sandals but not an extra tunic . . ."*
>
> *They went out and preached that people should repent. They drove out many demons and anointed many sick people with oil and healed them.* (Mark 6:7–9, 12–13)

The disciples were provided with a remarkable opportunity. They were going to field-test some of the lessons they had been taught in Jesus' ongoing evangelism seminar. Further, they were going out into the world with few provisions other than their own abilities and personalities, and the protection and guidance of their God. In a very real sense, disciples of today are provided with the same tools for reaching out to the world. The difference may be simply a matter of our willingness to fully exercise the use of those basic tools.

We have few details about the disciples' experiences on their first evangelistic mission. We are told, however, that they experienced some level of success in driving out demons and healing sick people (Mark 13:13). They also undoubtedly learned that with God's help they were capable of reaching out to the world that existed beyond their own small, select group. The disciples surely had many great stories to share enthusiastically with Jesus when they returned. It is likely that Jesus sat and listened intently as His disciples shared their stories of the road. Some of these were marked by success, and others could be filed in the category of "lessons learned the hard way." It is also probable that Jesus felt great pride in the accomplishments of His students as they began to learn firsthand what it felt like to share their newly awakened knowledge of God with excitement and enthusiasm.

In Mark 3:14 we also find Jesus communicating the core features of being an obedient follower, both of which have significant implications for a perspective on church culture: (1) His disciples are called to be with Him, and (2) they are called to be sent out.[1] For today's followers of Jesus Christ, being "with Him" means time spent in prayer, taking advantage of available teaching and preaching, and time studying and meditating on God's Word. But these activities are not enough. Disciples must also make themselves available to be sent out—out into the world for the purpose of making disciples and telling the world about the good news of Jesus Christ.

Jesus often taught the people and His disciples in the form of parables. These stories contain powerful theological messages and important lessons for living. The parable of the sower (Mark 4:1–20) primarily describes the varied manner in which people respond to the message of salvation. It also provides some insight into the results that can occur when mature Christians carry out their responsibility to share the gospel with others. The parable tells of the sower who spread seeds onto the ground. Some of the seed fell beside the road and was devoured by the birds (v. 4). Some of the seed fell on rocky ground, sprang up, and was parched by the sun and withered away (vv. 5–6). Some of the seed fell among the thorns, was choked, and yielded no crop (v. 7). Other seed fell into good soil, grew up, and yielded a bountiful crop (v. 8).

This parable has great implications for reaching the world for Christ. Jesus portrayed one of the hallmarks of "good soil" (mature Christians) as bearing fruit: thirty, sixty, and a hundredfold (multiplying themselves). For those individuals who wish to seriously follow the commands of Jesus, this means making a serious, ongoing commitment to making new disciples (multiplying ourselves).

Consider the following illustration of the multiplication principle:

If we are to be convinced of the need for spiritual reproduction in our churches, we need to understand and appreciate the principle of multiplication. It is basically the mathematical function of geometric progression. Envision a checkerboard. If you place one grain of wheat on the first square, two on the second square, then double that number for each square, how many grains of wheat would there be on the 64th square?

The answer, of course, is so astronomical that a number would be mind boggling. There would be enough wheat on that 64th square to cover the entire subcontinent of India several feet deep. This example simply shows the power of multiplication versus the slower method of addition. Project that illustration now to see the power of spiritual multiplication.

If your church had a member with the gift of evangelism who led an average of one person to Christ per week, who then joined your church, you would welcome an additional 52 members a year through the efforts of one church member. That is 520 people in ten years, considered excellent church growth.

But what if you had another member in your church who was so gifted that he led a person to Christ each day? If they all joined the church, that would mean 365 new members each year through the efforts of one person and you would have to have a new building program every three or so years, for you would have 3,652 new members in a decade.

But you also have another person in your church whose ministry is not so visible. She leads a person to Christ, then disciples that individual for a year, and the two of them each lead another to Christ, so at the end of two years you have four new members from this "slow" ministry. But they keep on reproducing. At the end of another year the four become eight, then 16 by the end of the fourth year. If this ministry continues, by the end of the 33rd year 8,589,934,592 people have been won to Christ and discipled, which is far over the population of the whole world![2]

Impossible? Probably so, but it is theoretically possible, for it shows the power of spiritual multiplication. It is an obvious ideal, and breakdowns can occur all through the process, but it is still the greatest potential the church has of reaching our world with the gospel in this generation.

Most of us acknowledge the relevance and importance of the Great Commission, but wonder how we can best accomplish this directive. We go back to Jesus' example. Gordon MacDonald identified four specific strategies that Jesus employed to interact with His community. These four strategies have relevance for today's culture: (1) Jesus entered the culture and played to its strengths and realities, (2) Jesus went first for the hearts of people, (3) Jesus started small, and (4) Jesus gave people a dream—the dream of a new kingdom.[3]

Jesus entered the culture and played to its strengths and realities. As Jesus moved about teaching and interacting with the people, He presented His message within the context and experience of His audience. For example, when Jesus called Peter, Andrew, James, and John to follow Him as disciples, He asked them to become "fishers of men" (Mark 3:4). This was particularly relevant, as these four potential disciples worked every day as professional fishermen. Jesus was talking their language. He was always culturally relevant.

Jesus went first for the hearts of people. Jesus looked into people's hearts and met them at the point of their greatest need. As Jesus talked privately with the woman at the well, He was well aware of her relationship problems and spiritual issues. His sensitivity and directness were responsive to the woman's situation and yet did not compromise a message of forgiveness that called her to repentance.

Jesus started small. Jesus did not operate within the context of a single location or even a megachurch. Although He often spoke to large groups of "seekers," Jesus frequently operated within the context of a small group. Although He delivered many significant messages to crowds, He also took the time to interact with individuals, building relationships and sharing God's good news. He built the church beginning with a small group (the disciples) and encouraged its members to practice the multiplication principle.

Jesus gave people a dream—the dream of a new kingdom. Jesus spoke often of a new kingdom, the place where God dwells, a place of justice, righteousness and infinite grace. This dream, which can only be a reality through a relationship with God, was once again responsive to the needs of the people.

What can we learn from the experiences of Jesus and the disciples as they interacted with their world? Several lessons emerge:

- There is a balance to be struck between "being with Him" and "being sent out." Both aspects of the disciples' spiritual life are critical. To "exercise" ourselves in the Word and in prayer without "getting into the game" by sharing the Word is a hollow spiritual experience. To depend upon our personal knowledge and resources without the support of prayer and biblical knowledge is an act of self-importance.

- Personal relationships are the starting point for reaching out.

- Reaching out is a learning process driven and supported by faith.

- One of the marks of a true disciple is the degree to which that individual is able to multiply himself or herself.

The Resulting Joy

The joy and peace that takes place in a new convert's life is often visible, especially during the early stages—but the decision to convert one's will to the will and lordship of Jesus Christ is always of eternal significance.

And I will do whatever you ask in my name, so that the Son may bring glory to the Father. You may ask me for anything in my name, and I will do it. (John 14:13–14)

On the last and greatest day of the Feast, Jesus stood and said in a loud voice, "If anyone is thirsty, let him come to me and drink. Whoever believes in me, as the Scripture has said, streams of living water will flow from within him." (John 7:37–38)

Even the angels will rejoice:

In the same way, I tell you, there is rejoicing in the presence of the angels of God over one sinner who repents. (Luke 15:10)

And you too will be fulfilled; that is, if you are a Christian participating in a life that is obedient to Christ, you will serve Him with your time, energy, and resources:

Even now the reaper draws his wages, even now he harvests the crop for eternal life, so that the sower and the reaper may be glad together. Thus the saying, 'One sows and another reaps' is true. I sent you to reap what you have not worked for. Others have done the hard work, and you have reaped the benefits of their labor. (John 4:36–38)

As Christians, we should be sharing Christ through our lifestyle and actions. Christ commanded such behavior. When people see you, are they interested in Christ?

Jesus answered, "I am the way and the truth and the life. No one comes to the Father except through me. If you really knew me, you would know my Father as well. From now on, you do know him and have seen him."

Philip said, "Lord, show us the Father and that will be enough for us."

Jesus answered: "Don't you know me, Philip, even after I have been among you such a long time? Anyone who has seen me has seen the Father. How can you say, 'Show us the Father'? Don't you believe that I am in the Father, and that the Father is in me? The words I say to you are not just my own. Rather, it is the Father, living in me, who is doing his work. Believe me when I say that I am in the Father and the Father is in me; or at least believe on the evidence of the miracles themselves. I tell you the truth, anyone who has faith in me will do what I have been doing. He will do even greater things than these, because I am going to the Father. And I will do whatever you ask in my name, so that the Son may bring glory to the Father. You may ask me for anything in my name, and I will do it.

"If you love me, you will obey what I command. And I will ask the Father, and he will give you another Counselor to be with you forever—the Spirit of truth. The world cannot accept him, because it neither sees him nor knows him. But you know him, for he lives with you and will be in you. I will not leave you as orphans; I will come to you. Before long, the world will not see me anymore, but you will see me. Because I live, you will also live. On that day you will realize that I am in my Father, and you are in me, and I am in you. Whoever has my commands and obeys them, he is the one who loves me. He who loves me will be loved by my Father, and I too will love him and show myself to him." (John 14:6–21)

We need to go beyond exemplifying Christ through our actions. Picture it as ways of putting into words, in a basic manner, what the Bible clearly states about the grounds for eternal life. As our peers, friends, relatives, and loved ones become curious, we need to be able to explain clearly why we live for Christ and how we became Christians.

There is often a tendency for us to think of "evangelism" in the third person; it is something "they" do out there somewhere at large rallies, by sharing Christ on a street corner, or by going on mission trips to foreign lands—things that "other" people do during their interactions with "strangers." Actually, the best evangelism occurs in the context of a relationship. Think for a moment about the people that you know and interact with on a regular basis, people who need to know Christ. Evangelism begins with each of us as individuals and our commitment to sharing the Good News.

On Sowing
(With thanks to RVL)

There are few things on earth that can make my skin crawl like the sight of Christians passing out pamphlets on street corners. The sight makes me uncomfortable for various reasons. I get uncomfortable partly because the pamphlets remind me of my waitressing days—when people would leave a very small tip on their table inside a very large brochure about Jesus. I also get uncomfortable with these pamphlet-passers because I dislike when people shove little papers at me when I'm going from place to place. My gut reaction to such a move is that it seems invasive, offensive, rude.

Still, I cannot deny the fact that many (quite possibly millions) have come to Christ as a result of a pamphlet. Some might even have come to Christ as a result of a small tip inside a large brochure. Although the pamphlet would be my last choice of a method to evangelize, it does work.

The beauty of the salvation message is that it is strong enough to transcend our human efforts and preferences. The Christian's task in this work of evangelism, then, is very simple. We do not need to be so methodical and calculated and prejudicial about how and when we evangelize. We must simply keep sowing seeds that hold the salvation message. Redemption is God's story, God's work. No matter what type of soil we have to work with, the seed remains the same. Wherever and however it is planted—even in the form of a pamphlet, life-changing potential is always found inside.

—Lisa Velthouse

 ## FAQ

Q. I'm not called to be a preacher. I don't have the gift of sharing with people. What can I do?

A. Recognize the comforting power of the Holy Spirit. Consider the following passage:

*But I tell you the truth: It is for your good that I am going
away. Unless I go away, the Counselor will not come to you;
but if I go, I will send him to you. When he comes, he will
convict the world of guilt in regard to sin and righteousness
and judgment: in regard to sin, because men do not believe
in me; in regard to righteousness, because I am going to the
Father, where you can see me no longer; and in regard to
judgment, because the prince of this world now stands
condemned.*

*I have much more to say to you, more than you can now
bear. But when he, the Spirit of truth, comes, he will guide
you into all truth. He will not speak on his own; he will speak
only what he hears, and he will tell you what is yet to come.*
(John 16:7–13)

Yes, we all have different functions in the Body of Christ, yet we
are all prepared to share Christ. This is our joy, out of our love for
Him. He promises to give you wisdom.

*If any of you lacks wisdom, he should ask God, who gives
generously to all without finding fault, and it will be given to
him.* (James 1:5)

Q. I am afraid of being rejected.
A. Christ was rejected. He was crucified. He chose to be
rejected so that we might receive Him. Yes, there may be occasions
when you are turned down or rejected as you deliver Christ's
message. But according to Christ's own words, this rejection will
only be temporary:

*Blessed are you when people insult you, persecute you and
falsely say all kinds of evil against you because of me.
Rejoice and be glad, because great is your reward in heaven,
for in the same way they persecuted the prophets who were
before you.* (Matthew 5:11–12)

And a few years after Christ died and was resurrected, the Apostle Paul wrote these powerful words of encouragement for our efforts on behalf of Christ:

> *But we have this treasure in jars of clay to show that this all-surpassing power is from God and not from us. We are hard pressed on every side, but not crushed; perplexed, but not in despair; persecuted, but not abandoned; struck down, but not destroyed. We always carry around in our body the death of Jesus, so that the life of Jesus may also be revealed in our body . . .*
>
> *We know that the one who raised the Lord Jesus from the dead will also raise us with Jesus and present us with you in his presence. All this is for your benefit, so that the grace that is reaching more and more people may cause thanksgiving to overflow to the glory of God.* (2 Corinthians 4:7–10, 14–15).

Reaction and Reflection

1. Think back. How did you first become aware of Jesus Christ? Who was the person who introduced you to Him?

2. Describe your salvation experience—Who, How, and Where?

   a.   Who?

b.   How?

c.   Where?

3. Think about your possibilities for evangelism. Who are some of
    the people and in what places might you become involved in
    evangelism?

Suggested Readings and Resources

Bickel, B., and Stan Jantz. *Bruce & Stan's Pocket Guide to Sharing Your Faith*
(Pocket Guide). Eugene, OR: Harvest House Publishers, Inc, 2000.

Bright, B. *Witnessing Without Fear*. Nashville: Thomas Nelson, 1992.

————. *Five Steps to Sharing Your Faith*. Peachtree City, GA: New Life
Publications, 2002.

Graham, F. *It's Who You Know: The One Relationship that Makes All the
Difference*. Nashville: Thomas Nelson, 2002.

————. *The Name of Jesus*. Nashville: Thomas Nelson, 2002.

Laurie, G. *How to Share Your Faith*. Carol Stream, IL: Tyndale House
Publishers, 1999.

Little, P. *How to Give Away Your Faith*. Downers Grove, IL: Intervarsity Press, 1989.

Lucado, M. *A Love Worth Giving: Living in the Overflow of God's Love*. Nashville: W Publishing Group, 2002.

Mittelberg, M., Lee Strobel, and Bill Hybels. *Becoming a Contagious Christian*. Grand Rapids, MI: Zondervan, 1995.

Stowell, J. *Simply Jesus: Experiencing the One Your Heart Longs For*. Portland, OR: Multnomah Publishers, 2002.

Strobel, L., and Bill Hybels. *Inside the Unchurched Harry and Mary*. Grand Rapids, MI: Zondervan, 1993.

Warren, R. *The Purpose-Driven Church*. Grand Rapids, MI: Zondervan, 1995.

Endnotes

1. From a lecture by Dr. Grant Osborne as part of the "New Testament Survey" course taught through Trinity Evangelical Divinity School.

2. Billy Graham Evangelical Association, Center of Strategic Evangelism. http://www.gospelcom.net/bgc/ise/ (accessed August 7, 2007).

3. Gordon MacDonald, "Atmospheric Influences," *Leadership Journal* 20 (Winter 1999): 3.

introducing
Christ

sharing the gospel message

For this son of mine was dead and is alive again; he was lost and is found.'

He said to them: *"It is not for you to know the times or dates the Father has set by his own authority. But you will receive power when the Holy Spirit comes on you; and you will be my witnesses in Jerusalem, and in all Judea and Samaria, and to the ends of the earth."*

(Acts 1:7–8)

a night shift memory:
witnessing the rejection of witnessing

After sharing the plan of salvation with the Chicago-area janitor, at his request I asked, "Is this what you need in your life?" He thought a minute and blurted out, "Nah! You know what I really need right now, Jerry?" Before I could answer, he added, "A good woman." He put away his cart and went immediately to his "Bondo™-ed" bald-tired Monte Carlo.

This snaggled-toothed, tattooed, greasy-haired' depressed janitor in the drab blue uniform had begged me to tell him about Christ. He wanted to know what it meant to become a Christian. We had become acquainted with each other over the months—I usually worked evenings and he would pause for coffee while leaning against my doorframe. In time, he began to do some real soul searching.

His questions weren't about his chain-smoking breaks or his drinking binges. Although those are health concerns, at best they were symptoms of a deeper problem—a void in his heart and life. After failed marriages he had temporarily vowed to give up dating. He had even curbed late-night television marathons. He was trying to "get his life in order." He wanted to know, "What makes you tick, Jerry?"

His direct questions were rare and refreshing. Not many people have approached me with the simple honest question, "Tell me, what does it take to become a Christian? I might be interested."

That evening I pulled out my Bible, an original NIV brown hardback that looked worn before its time. My little chart on witnessing was taped inside the cover. It contained the key questions to address, a clear Scripture to back up the answer, and the page number to find the Scripture. Within a few minutes he thanked me for clarifying the issues, and said that he understood. At that point, I had witnessed. He had heard and understood. And he had rejected the message.

As the following chapter outlines, there are ways in which the gospel message can be shared that covers the important issues. The steps of decision are firmly based in the words of Christ found in the New Testament. Keep in mind, however, that no matter how clearly and politely you present the plan of salvation, or how articulate and creative you are, some people will accept and some will reject. That important decision is between them and God.

As we saw earlier in the book, God, in the form of the Holy Spirit, is present in this world. It remains a mystery how the Holy Spirit operates in people's lives as they become Christians.

Regardless of these different perspectives, people need to have a clear understanding of the plan of salvation—both for those deciding to accept Christ, and for those wanting to share His message.

introducing
Christ

sharing the gospel message

 ## Consider the Source

All authority in heaven and on earth has been given to me. Therefore go and make disciples of all nations, baptizing them in the name of the Father and of the Son and of the Holy Spirit, and teaching them to obey everything I have commanded you. And surely I am with you always, to the very end of the age. (Matthew 28:18–20)

Understand the Need

We all know and believe that sharing Christ should be an enjoyable and common aspect of one's Christian life. And often these efforts result in new converts to Christianity. As believers in Jesus Christ, we should have a strong desire to share the gospel with our loved ones, friends, neighbors, and coworkers—all the people with whom we interact on a daily basis. For many of us, however, the prospect of sharing the gospel with someone is frightening. Witnessing is an important responsibility for all believers—the world is in desperate need of what God can provide. But uncertainty about how to clearly communicate the salvation message and trepidation about the prospect of ridicule, failure, humiliation, or rejection are significant roadblocks to witnessing for many believers.

In this chapter, we hope to provide you with new confidence about your ability—provided through the power of the Holy Spirit—to share the powerful message of God's grace and forgiveness. Further, we believe that with practice, commitment, and the guiding of the Holy Spirit, witnessing can become a lifestyle rather than an event. The remainder of this chapter looks at several ways to effectively share Christ's plan of salvation.

Desiring to Share Christ

In the 1960s, playwright John Guare wrote *Six Degrees of Separation*. This play tells the story of a young man who, claiming to be the son of actor Sidney Poitier, becomes acquainted with a well-to-do New York City art dealer and his wife. The play focuses on the relationship that evolves between these individuals. Through their experiences, we learn how closely each of us is connected with other inhabitants of planet earth.

A "degree of separation" in this context is an acquaintance who connects you to someone you have never met. For example, Tom and Mary are friends. Tom has another acquaintance named John who doesn't know Mary. There is one degree of separation between Tom and Mary, and two degrees of separation between Mary and John. In theory, there are only six degrees of separation between each of us and any other person in the entire world—a mind-boggling thought. Although this theory would be virtually impossible to prove, it does have a strong backing from several prominent mathematicians.[1]

This theory has taken on a life of its own. For example, college students created a contest called "The Kevin Bacon Game."[2] This game, named after the actor, involves connecting any other actor or actress to Kevin Bacon using the principle of six degrees of separation. So, for example,

- The actor Sean Connery was in the movie *League of Extraordinary Gentlemen* (2003) with Stuart Townsend.

- Stuart Townsend was in the movie *Trapped* (2002) with Kevin Bacon.

- So, Sean Connery and Kevin Bacon are separated by "two degrees."

The possibilities are endless. Suppose that someone you know, by some unusual circumstances, knows someone who knows an African pygmy. By this chain of unlikely acquaintances, you are connected to the African pygmy (and only separated by three degrees).

You may be asking yourself, "What in the world does this have to do with witnessing?" Good question. The answer, however, is one that you may already know. For example, consider Jesus' direct and critically important commandment to His disciples (and to us):

"But you will receive power when the Holy Spirit comes on you; and you will be my witnesses in Jerusalem, and in all Judea and Samaria, and to the ends of the earth." (Acts 1:8)

For many of us, the "ends of the earth" command is satisfied by giving financial support to missionaries. These missionaries travel to foreign lands on our behalf to preach the gospel and to bring others into a relationship with Jesus Christ. The concept of "six degrees of separation" places a whole new slant on the idea of reaching forth to make disciples of the whole world. Stated in a global fashion, we are only six degrees of separation away from reaching the entire population of the world with the gospel of Jesus Christ! Imagine it. I must begin the process by sharing the salvation message with those people that I know. Then, if they share the message with people that they know, and they share the message with people that they know . . . But, it begins with each of us as individuals. Do we have the desire and the commitment to share God's message with our friends and acquaintances? A world for Christ is in the balance.

Who is Your Target Audience?

Think about all of the people you know. It is very likely that all of us know a wide variety of people who have never established a personal relationship with Jesus Christ. And although we know how critically important it is for these friends, loved ones, neighbors, and coworkers to have a relationship with Jesus Christ, we often don't feel a sense of urgency in sharing this message that has eternal significance. To begin the process of witnessing, we must first have an appreciation and understanding of our target audience: what are they thinking and feeling? Consider the following description of the unbelieving:

> We must first understand the basic nature of the unbelieving friends we are seeking to reach. Knowing their spiritual composition is a great help in understanding who they are from God's viewpoint and what is likely to be their response to the spiritual truth.

Blind
First, regardless of how intelligent or enlightened your acquaintance may appear, he or she is blinded to the truth of the gospel. *"But even if our gospel is veiled, it is veiled to those who are perishing, whose minds the god of this age has blinded, who do not believe, lest the light of the gospel of the glory of Christ, who is the image of God, should shine on them"* (2 Corinthians 4:3, 4). Until a person is regenerated (born again) by the Spirit of God, he or she remains in spiritual darkness. Persuading your friend of the deity and reality of Christ and personal need for the Savior is not an educational endeavor. That is why simple logic and reasoning alone won't bring an individual into a relationship with Christ. Satan, the "god of this age," is covertly at work doing all he can to keep the unbeliever in the dark concerning sin and salvation.

Captive
Not only are our non-Christian friends blind to the truth, but they are captives of the Evil One. Jesus said, *"Most assuredly, I say to you, whoever commits sin is a slave of sin"* (John 8:34). Paul wrote Timothy that sharing with unbelievers

means presenting the truth so that *"they may come to their senses and escape the snare of the devil, having been taken captive by him to do his [Satan's] will"* (2 Timothy 2:26). In essence, the unbeliever is a spiritual prisoner of war. This is why there is often a hint of hostility from the unbeliever when we present the good news. Satan does not want to lose his mastery over fallen men and women. Regardless of how decent and honorable and appealing our friends may appear on the surface, unless Christ is Lord of their lives, they are spiritual hostages of the adversary.

Dead

Above all, your friends without Christ are spiritually dead. *"And you he made alive who were dead in trespasses and sins, in which you once walked according to the course of this world, according to the prince of the power of the air, the spirit who now works in the sons of disobedience"* (Ephesians 2:1, 2). Spiritually dead people are those who are unresponsive to the spiritual light and truth. They are dead in spirit toward God. The life of Christ has yet to shine in their hearts. Though they may enjoy the "good life" or be the "life of the party," they are separated and alienated from the source of eternal and abundant life, Jesus Christ.[3]

It is critically important to have a heart for those who have not yet come into a relationship with Jesus Christ. We are called to care.

Common Sense Preparation

It is important to communicate the message of salvation in a clear and concise manner. Being prepared for the prospect of witnessing is good common sense. Consider the following steps of preparation that will help get you ready to witness:

1. Tape a scriptural reference guide inside the cover of your Bible. Photocopy these, or simply write them on the inside cover of your Bible.

ave you ever really considered—that you are Jesus Christ to the people you know? You and I are his instruments standing in the place of the Lord Jesus Christ, beseeching others to be reconciled to God. To me that is a grabber. As you and I go to work, walk down the street, talk to our roommates, visit over the back fence, we are in face to face conversation with people for whom Christ died. We may even be the last link in the chain that stretches out to them from the throne of God, the chain God forged to bring them faith. There may be no one else they know who can tell them God's message of reconciliation. And that carries with it a solemn responsibility. The privilege of it as well, it seems to me, is overwhelming.

Paul Little
How to Give Away Your Faith [4]

2. Write the page numbers next to the Scriptures found in the reference block. It is also helpful to mark them in your Bible with a highlighter. Turn to them as you share.

3. Write the page number of the next point on the bottom of the page of that preceding point. For example, after turning to John 3:3 and sharing the essence of that Scripture, glance at the bottom of the page, see the written number, and quickly turn to the next point—Acts 17:30. This practice helps to maintain people's interest. You don't waste their time while you are looking for Scriptures.

4. Familiarize yourself with these Scriptures and how to best explain each one clearly and succinctly.

Salvation Scriptures

___Born again	John 3:3
___Repentance	Acts 17:30
___Belief	John 3:36
___Confession	Romans 10:9
___Assurance	Revelation 3:20

Key Scriptures

___Life	John 10:10
___Sin	Romans 3:23
___Penalty	Romans 6:23
___Love	John 3:14–17
___Way/Truth/Life	John 14:6
___Not Perish	2 Peter 3:9

5. Rehearse your presentation. As you begin to share the need for "receiving" Christ, stress its importance. People can realize their need to be born again, to repent of sins, and to confess Christ, yet still not be saved. Salvation occurs when they personally receive Christ into their hearts. You can easily and vividly illustrate this for them. The following object lesson might help:

> Hold out a pen, and then announce that you are giving it to the person to whom you are witnessing. Ask, "Do you feel like this pen is yours? No? Well, then, what must you do to actually make this pen yours?" Have the person actually reach out and take the pen. The taking symbolizes receiving. We must receive Christ into our hearts.

6. Conclude with a time of prayer, inviting this individual to personally receive Christ by praying with you. The decision is that person's, not yours. The Holy Spirit works in the lives of people in various ways. If someone chooses not to accept Christ, pray for that person. Let him or her know you hope that one day soon he or she will have a clear understanding of Christ's love and will accept Him as Savior. If this person wants to accept Christ, ask him or her to repeat after you as you lead the individual through the responses to the needs you discussed (i.e., repent, believe, confess, and receive).

The most important preparation you can make for witnessing is prayer. Integral to the process of witnessing is an invitation for the Holy Spirit to guide your words, actions, and responses.

The Importance of Transition

Have you ever entered a discussion and been unable to bring it around to a point where you actually shared the plan of salvation—even though you wanted to? For example, if a friend who loves computers has a broken relationship with a girlfriend, perhaps it's a problem of perspective and/or priorities. If he admits an obsession with Web use, he is beginning to see the importance of perspective. You might also ask him how he gains perspective on other key life choices. This topic has numerous overlaps with spiritual decisions, and the key decision of serving Christ.

When you have been in similar discussions, what are some of the things that prohibited you from making that move to spiritual questions, and ultimately the question to become a Christian? These situations become easier when you can begin to see "eternal priorities and temporal concerns." When your will is sincerely that of the Father (God), He makes available the added strength and wisdom to handle various situations. The following Scriptures represent God's promises of divine assistance.

> *But to those whom God has called, both Jews and Greeks, Christ [is] the power of God and the wisdom of God. For the foolishness of God is wiser than man's wisdom, and the weakness of God is stronger than man's strength.*

> *Brothers, think of what you were when you were called. Not many of you were wise by human standards; not many were influential; not many were of noble birth. But God chose the foolish things of the world to shame the wise; God chose the weak things of the world to shame the strong. He chose the lowly things of this world and the despised things—and the things that are not—to nullify the things that are.* (1 Corinthians 1:24–28)

> *But he said to me, "My grace is sufficient for you, for my power is made perfect in weakness." Therefore I will boast all the more gladly about my weaknesses, so that Christ's power may rest on me.* (2 Corinthians 12:9)

> *Our gospel came to you not simply with words, but also with power, with the Holy Spirit and with deep conviction. You know how we lived among you for your sake.* (1 Thessalonians 1:5)

For God did not give us a spirit of timidity, but a spirit of power, of love and of self-discipline. (2 Timothy 1:7)

If any of you lacks wisdom, he should ask God, who gives generously to all without finding fault, and it will be given to him. (James 1:5)

Our Lives as Testimony

One of the most dramatic conversions described in the New Testament is that of the Apostle Paul. Prior to coming to know Christ, Paul (then known as Saul) was an active and vicious persecutor of those who believed in Christ. Consider his testimony:

I am a Jew born in Tarsus of Cicilia, but brought up in this city. Under Gamaliel I was thoroughly trained in the law of our fathers and was just as zealous for God as any of you are today. I persecuted the followers of this Way to their death, arresting both men and women and throwing them into prison, as also the high priest and all the Council can testify. I even obtained letters from them to their brothers in Damascus, and went there to bring these people as prisoners to Jerusalem to be punished.

About noon as I came near to Damascus, suddenly a bright light from heaven flashed around me. I fell to the ground and heard a voice say to me, "Saul! Saul! Why do you persecute me?"

"Who are you, Lord?" I asked.

"I am Jesus of Nazareth, whom you are persecuting," he replied. My companions saw the light, but they did not understand the voice of him who was speaking to me.

"What shall I do, Lord?" I asked.

"Get up," the Lord said, "and go into Damascus. There you will be told all that you have been assigned to do." My companions led me by the hand into Damascus, because the brilliance of the light had blinded me.

A man named Ananias came to see me. He was a devout observer of the law and highly respected by all the Jews living there. He stood beside me and said, "Brother Saul, receive your sight!" And at that very moment I was able to see him.

Then he said, "The God of our fathers has chosen you to know his will and to see the Righteous One and to hear words from his mouth. You will be his witness to all men of what you have seen and heard. And now what are you waiting for? Get up, be baptized and wash your sins away, calling on his name."

When I returned to Jerusalem and was praying at the temple, I fell into a trance, and saw the Lord speaking. "Quick!" he said to me. "Leave Jerusalem immediately, because they will not accept your testimony about me."

"Lord," I replied, "these men know that I went from one synagogue to another to imprison and beat those who believe in you. And when the blood of your martyr Stephen was shed, I stood there giving my approval and guarding the clothes of those who were killing him."

Then the Lord said to me, "Go; I will send you far away to the Gentiles." (Acts 22:3–21)

Being God's Witness

Some people believe that a person's religion is a personal matter and therefore Christians should not talk about their faith to others. But the Bible commands us to be witnesses for Jesus Christ.

Bill Bright of Campus Crusade defined a witness as any Christian who bears testimony of the death, burial, and resurrection of Jesus Christ by life and by lips. In other words, a witness is one who first receives the gospel himself, and then proclaims that truth to others. A person cannot teach or testify to a truth that he or she does not personally believe and practice. The writer of Psalm 107 wrote, "Let the redeemed of the Lord say so."

Jesus, in Matthew 28, gave the following command, "Go and make disciples of all nations . . ." The word that is used to describe Christians going forth to witness for Jesus Christ is *evangelism*.

Archbishop William Temple offers two definitions of "evangelism" that I especially like:

Evangelism is proclaiming the Good News of salvation by grace through faith toward the goal of making disciples of Jesus Christ, resulting in their incorporation into the church.

To evangelize is to present Christ in the power of the Holy Spirit that men will come to put their trust in God through Him, to accept Him as their Savior, and to serve Him as their King in the fellowship of His church.

There is a common theme. Evangelism is sharing with people about Jesus Christ and the salvation He offers to all humankind.

—Jim "Umfundisi" Lo

In the book *Lifestyle Evangelism* by Joe Aldrich, we are encouraged to develop our own story of coming to know Christ into a personal testimony that we can share with others. The Acts 3 model described above illustrates the power of Paul's personal testimony. These are the components of a personal testimony:

- **My life before knowing Christ**

  Describe the challenges and temptations that you faced before knowing Jesus Christ as your personal Savior.

- **How I became aware of my need for Christ**

  Describe the process (people, experiences, situations) that moved you toward a realization that you needed to have God in your life.

- **How I received Christ**

  What happened at that moment when you received Christ into your heart? Who was there? Where were you? Who was the person who introduced you into God's family?

- **What Christ is doing in my life**

  Now that you have accepted Jesus Christ as your Savior, what types of life changes have you noticed?[5]

Following God's Call to Witness

Now an angel of the Lord said to Philip, "Go south to the road—the desert road—that goes down from Jerusalem to Gaza." So he started out, and on his way he met an Ethiopian eunuch, an important official in charge of all the treasury of Candace, queen of the Ethiopians. This man had gone to Jerusalem to worship, and on his way home was sitting in his chariot reading the book of Isaiah the prophet. The Spirit told Philip, "Go to that chariot and stay near it."

Then Philip ran up to the chariot and heard the man reading Isaiah the prophet. "Do you understand what you are reading?" Philip asked.

"How can I," he said, "unless someone explains it to me?" So he invited Philip to come up and sit with him . . . Then Philip began with that very passage of Scripture and told him the good news about Jesus. (Acts 8:26–31, 35)

As a believer in Jesus Christ, there will be times and opportunities for you to share the gospel with others. Just as important as being prepared and knowing how to share the good news about Jesus is having a heart that is willing to give testimony. Just as Philip eagerly followed the direction of the Holy Spirit, we too must be ready and willing to go where God directs. Are you ready *and* willing?

2·6·2: A Method for Sharing the Gospel

The organization "Dare 2 Share" focuses its energies on teaching high school and college students how to effectively identify opportunities to share their faith. Dare 2 Share members also provide a strategy for sharing the gospel in a logical manner. The 2-6-2 technique is an evangelism tactic that has been tested and proven to be an extremely effective tool in sharing the gospel. It involves asking two (2) personalized questions, sharing six (6) key principles from the Bible, and asking two (2) closing questions.

2 Personalized Questions:

Begin by asking a friend, family member, neighbor, or stranger two questions. Samples include:

- Would you mind if I shared my spiritual beliefs with you?
- What do you think a person has to do to get to heaven?
- Would you mind if I shared with you what the Bible says a person has to do?
- How has 9/11 impacted your view of life and death?
- Would you mind if I told you why I'm not afraid to die?
- Do you know for sure that you will go to heaven when you die?
- If I could tell you in less than two minutes how you could know for sure, would that be good news?
- What's your religious background?
- Who do think Jesus was? (God, man, good teacher, lunatic, etc.)
- May I share with you who I believe He was and why He died on the cross?

6 Penetrating Points:

After asking two questions, students then share the six points of the gospel:

God created us to be with Him. *(Genesis 1:26—Then God said, "Let us make man in our image, in our likeness . . .")* God's desire in creating humankind was that we would live in a perfect paradise and enjoy perfect fellowship with Him.

Our sin separates us from God. *(Genesis 6:5–6—The LORD saw how great man's wickedness on the earth had become, and that every inclination of the thoughts of his heart was only evil all the time. The LORD was grieved that he had made man on the earth, and his heart was filled with pain.)* The wrong things that we have done (sins) have placed a barrier between humankind and our Creator.

Sin cannot be removed by good deeds. *(Titus 3:5—He saved us, not because of righteous things we had done, but because of his mercy. He saved us through the washing of rebirth and renewal by the Holy Spirit.)* There is nothing we can do through our own efforts that can restore our broken relationship with God.

Paying the price for sin, Jesus died and rose again. *(1 Corinthians 15:3–4—For what I received I passed on to you as of first importance: that Christ died for our sins according to the Scriptures, that he was buried, that he was raised on the third day according to the Scriptures.)* Jesus came to earth and lived a perfect life, died a horrible death, and rose from the grave to pay the price for all of the sins of humankind.

Everyone who trusts in Him *alone* has eternal life. *(John 6:47—I tell you the truth, he who believes has everlasting life.)* By simply placing our trust in Jesus' death and Resurrection as our only hope of salvation, we receive the free gift of salvation.

Life that's eternal means we will be with Jesus forever in heaven. *(Revelation 22:5—There will be no more night. They will not need the light of a lamp or the light of the sun, for the Lord God will give them light. And they will reign for ever and ever.)* Those who have placed their trust in Christ have forgiveness of sins and a restored relationship with God forever.

2 Penetrating Closers:

After sharing the six points, ask the final two questions:

1. **Does that make sense?** Make absolutely certain that the person completely understands the gospel. If he or she doesn't, simply go back over the six points and clarify.

2. **Will you trust in Jesus right now as your only hope of going to heaven?**

If the person says yes, then he or she has just become a believer. Remember that praying a prayer is not what saves a person, but if that person wants to express trust in Christ through a prayer, you can use the following as a sample:

"Dear Father, I know that I'm a sinner. I realize that my good deeds will never get me into heaven. Right now I believe that Jesus died in my place for my sins. I trust in Him alone to forgive me for all of my sins. Thank you for your free gift of eternal life."[6]

On Remembering

Around the holidays each year, my dad and my uncles pass time around the Christmas tree by reminiscing and reliving the events of their childhoods. They talk about baseball games, boxing matches, and birds that they kept in a shed behind their house. They throw their heads back and laugh when they talk about that time when my two aunts tried to bite through a pair of jeans that was stuck in a bicycle chain. They laugh and laugh, and the whole family laughs with them.

There's nothing like a good story, and this is precisely why witnessing can be such a powerful tool. To share one's faith, to "bear witness" is to give evidence that supports an idea, a truth. There is no evidence of the truth of Christ that is more powerful than the individual stories that He has given His children. Every Christian has a compelling story of forgiveness and grace and truth to share, no matter how new or old their faith. Every Christian has a story with the potential to compel millions—*millions*—into a relationship with Christ.

Sharing the message of the gospel is as simple as reminiscing about birds in a shed or blue jeans in a bicycle chain. To share the gospel is to share your story, to remember where you used to be, and to show others how God brought you to where you are today. There's nothing like a good story, and you've got one. When's the last time you shared it?

—Lisa Velthouse

 Reaction and Reflection

1. Make a list of the people in your life who, as far as you know, still need to establish a relationship with Jesus Christ.

2. Stop now and pray for these individuals.

   • Pray that they might have hearts that are prepared to hear God's message to them.

- Pray that God might use you to share the gospel.
- Pray that you might be ready and prepared.

3. What is your story? Write out your personal testimony.
   My life before knowing Christ:

   How I became aware of my need for Christ:

   How I received Christ:

   What Christ is doing in my life:

4. Find a friend and practice sharing your testimony.

Suggested Readings and Resources

Books

Aldrich, J. *Lifestyle Evangelism: Learning to Open Your Life to Those Around You*. Portland, OR: Multnomah Publications, 1999.

Bright, B. *Witnessing Without Fear*. Nashville: Thomas Nelson, 1992.

Graham, F. *It's Who You Know: The One Relationship That Makes All the Difference*. Nashville: Thomas Nelson, 2002.

———. *The Name of Jesus*. Nashville: Thomas Nelson, 2002.

Lucado, M. *A Love Worth Giving: Living in the Overflow of God's Love*. Nashville: W Publishing Group, 2002.

Stowell, J. *Simply Jesus: Experiencing the One Your Heart Longs For*. Portland, OR: Multnomah Publishers, 2002.

Other Resources

Campus Crusade. http://www.ccciorg (accessed August 6, 2007). Check out the Evangelism Toolbox for excellent witnessing resources.

Dare 2 Share. http:// www.dare2share.org (accessed August 6, 2007). Excellent resources on the 2-6-2 strategy and other issues and approaches in witnessing.

Endnotes

1. Steven Strogatz and Duncan Watts are two mathematicians who have built a mathematical model based on the six degrees of separation. "How does 'six degrees of separation' work?" Available online at http://www.cs.cornell.edu /News/6degreesofseparation (accessed August 6, 2007).

2. "6-Degrees-of-Separation Married by Math." Available online at http://www.members. fortunecity.com/jonhays/6degrees.htm (accessed August 6, 2007).

3. "How Can I Better Understand the People with Whom I Want to Share My Faith?" InTouch Ministries. Available at http://www.intouch.org/myintouch/ exploring/bible_says/witnessing/audience.html (accessed August 6, 2007).

4. Paul Little, *How to Give Away Your Faith* (Downers Grove, IL: InterVarsity Press, 1989).

5. Joe Aldrich, *Lifestyle Evangelism: Learning to Open Your Life to Those Around You* (Portland, OR: Multnomah Publications, 1999).

6. "2-6-2 Method" materials from Dare 2 Share Available online at http://www.dare2share.org/dare2share (accessed August 6, 2007).

growing in faith

the process of discipleship

As Jesus walked beside the Sea of Galilee, he saw Simon and his brother Andrew casting a net into the lake, for they were fishermen. *"Come, follow me,"* Jesus said, *"and I will make you fishers of men."* At once they left their nets and followed him.

(Mark 1:16–18)

a teaching memory:
the relevance of scripture

Accountability and spiritual growth can occur in many ways. Sometimes they begin at serious life crossroads. An encounter with one of my students illustrates this principle.

It was an unusually balmy, smoggy California afternoon when one of my senior students—I'll call him Joe—dropped in unannounced to talk. One of the real joys of teaching is the serendipitous time with students—especially those you've had the opportunity to mentor. This particular student considered me a key person in his college life, even though he rarely initiated conversation, and had never stopped in without an appointment.

The chat turned to rambling. As the day wore on, I imagined that the late-afternoon Friday traffic was undoubtedly backing up from Redlands to Pasadena. I finally forced the question. "Joe, is there something else you want to talk about?"

"Uh . . . Why do you ask?"

"You seem to be a bit preoccupied about something. Nervous. You're even sweating. And, we've had a rather disconnected chat for the past hour and a half. This isn't like you."

His demeanor changed. He actually settled down a bit and collapsed in the shabby office chair. His posture went from nervous and anxious to that of a deflated balloon. The game was over and he was ready to talk, really talk.

"Prof, how did you know?"

Mystified, I stabbed at a guess. "You were obviously wanting to address something."

"But, how did you know what I was dealing with?"

About all I could add was, "Joe, you'll need to help out here. Why did you think I knew?" Actually, I was clueless.

He then sat up and said, "You hit my problem on the head with your letter." Earlier that week I had mailed him a letter asking about his class performance. He was usually a good student, but his grades were slipping to borderline failure.

"Well, I sent that letter because it was obvious that you were having a tough time."

He nearly cut me off. "But how did you know exactly what my problem was?" I then asked him to be more specific.

"Dr. Pattengale, that Scripture at the end was just what I needed. I want you to know that my girlfriend and I have asked for forgiveness for being too physical and we also plan to get engaged as soon as I can afford a ring."

Now I was really curious. "I'm not sure I follow you. I sign all my letters with that Scripture."

His face began to drain of color. "You do?"

"Joe, do you have the letter?" I asked. He pulled the wrinkled letter from his backpack and handed it to me. At the bottom was . . . I winced. "Oh no," I said as reality hit. "I'm not sure why I did this, but I put *2 Tim. 2:22* instead of *2 Tim. 2:2*."

During my years on faculty at Azusa Pacific University, I signed most of my correspondence with the reference 2 Timothy 2:2: "You have heard me teach many things that have been confirmed by many reliable witnesses. Teach these great truths to trustworthy people who are able to pass them on to others" (NLT).

In this case, I had mistakenly put 2 Timothy 2:22: "Now flee from youthful lusts" (NASB).

At first, Joe was embarrassed and frustrated. I was wondering how many other times I had made that mistake.

In the end, we prayed about the situation and I was able to help him establish an accountability plan. Things worked out in his relationship with his girl and, in time, we could chuckle about this incident.

Our relationship, coupled with four years as teacher and student, facilitated this time of growth. Discipleship—or as it's often called today, mentorship—takes a commitment. It involves an investment of time and it involves priorities.

Joe and I had a faculty/student relationship. I had mentored him in some key areas, not only in the academic realm, but in the spiritual realm as well.

growing in faith

the process of discipleship

 Consider the Source

As Jesus walked beside the Sea of Galilee, he saw Simon and his brother Andrew casting a net into the lake, for they were fishermen. "Come, follow me," Jesus said, "and I will make you fishers of men." At once they left their nets and followed him.

When he had gone a little farther, he saw James son of Zebedee and his brother John in a boat, preparing their nets. Without delay he called them, and they left their father Zebedee in the boat with the hired men and followed him. (Mark 1:16–20)

Once again Jesus went out beside the lake. A large crowd came to him, and he began to teach them. As he walked along, he saw Levi son of Alphaeus sitting at the tax collector's booth. "Follow me," Jesus told him, and Levi got up and followed him. (Mark 2:13–14)

Jesus went up on a mountainside and called to him those he wanted, and they came to him. He appointed twelve— designating them apostles—that they might be with him and that he might send them out to preach and to have authority to drive out demons. (Mark 3:13–15)

Understand the Need

What does it mean to be a disciple? We are all familiar with the twelve men known as disciples who traveled with Jesus: a unique group of men who had the privilege of interacting directly with Jesus on a daily basis. Together they shared an intimate time of personal contact with the Son of God. During their time together, Jesus taught and guided the disciples in preparation for the time that He would leave them and they would carry on the work of spreading the gospel. (Refer to the fictionalized letter that follows. It highlights the humanity and personalities of the people Jesus chose to be His disciples in ministry).

As Christians, we also have been invited to be disciples. This invitation includes a responsibility to live in a way that glorifies God, to exercise the "disciplines" of daily living that connect us to God (e.g., prayer, Bible study, the use of our time and resources), to share the good news of salvation with the world, and to assist others in their journey toward spiritual maturity. The Gospel of Mark provides a series of snapshots which reveal the basic principles of effective discipleship. Through a study of Mark, we are introduced to the daily experiences of the twelve disciples chosen by Jesus. We watch them as they grow in their understanding. We also are permitted to view the questions, uncertainties, disbelief, and weaknesses of those twelve who were the closest friends of Jesus. This legacy provides us with great lessons for living as we grow in our role as disciples of Jesus Christ.

Jordan Management Consultants

To: Jesus, Son of Joseph
            Woodcrafter's Carpenter Shop
            Nazareth 25922

From: Jordan Management Consultants

Dear Sir:

Thank you for submitting the resumes of the twelve men you have picked for managerial positions in your new organization. All of them have now taken our battery of tests; and we have not only run the results through our computer, but also arranged personal interviews for each of them with our psychologist and vocational aptitude consultant. The profiles and all tests are included, and you will want to study each of them carefully.

As part of our service, we make some general comments for your guidance, much as an auditor will include some general statements. This is given as a result of staff consultation, and comes without any additional fee. It is the staff opinion that most of your nominees are lacking in background, education and vocational aptitude for the type of enterprise you are undertaking. They do not have the team concept. We would recommend that you continue your search for persons of experience in managerial ability and proven capability.

Simon Peter is emotionally unstable and given to fits of temper. Andrew has absolutely no qualities of leadership. The two brothers, James and John, the sons of Zebedee, place personal interest above company loyalty. Thomas demonstrates a questioning attitude that would tend to undermine morale. We feel that it is our duty to tell you that Matthew has been blacklisted by the Greater Jerusalem Better Business Bureau; James, the son of Alphaeus, and Thaddaeus definitely have radical leanings, and they both registered a high score on the manic-depressive scale.

One of the candidates, however, shows great potential. He is a man of ability and resourcefulness, meets people well, has a keen business mind, and has contacts in high places. He is highly motivated, ambitious, and responsible. We recommend Judas Iscariot as your controller and right-hand man. All of the other profiles are self-explanatory. We wish you every success in your new venture.

Sincerely,

Jordan Management Consultants[1]

When Jesus Calls

As Jesus called those whom He had chosen to be His disciples, they responded in faith. The connection between faith and obedience is a strong one. Obedience is faith in action. The events surrounding the calling of the disciples involved three specific ingredients:

- A heart inspired by faith

- A calling by Jesus to follow Him

- An obedient response

We too should seek to follow Jesus when He calls. Faith requires an obedient response.

—J. Bradley Garner

What does it mean to be a "disciple" of Jesus Christ in the twenty-first century? In September 1999, a group of 450 theologians from 70 countries gathered in England for the "First International Consultation on Discipleship." This group affirmed the critical importance of discipleship and the following definition:

Discipleship is a process that takes place within accountable relationships over a period of time for the purpose of bringing believers to spiritual maturity in Christ.

This definition raises two critical aspects of the process of becoming a disciple:

1. Growth in our own personal relationship with Jesus Christ
2. Entering into relationships with others to facilitate and encourage their movement toward spiritual maturity[2]

Both are required . . . Neither can be ignored.

Your Development as a Disciple

In this chapter, we will examine the developmental process of becoming a disciple of Jesus Christ. Rick Warren is the pastor of Saddleback Church in Park Forest, California. In his book *The Purpose-Driven Church*, he has conceptualized the development of a disciple as running around a baseball diamond.[3] This model reinforces the fact that spiritual growth usually occurs in a sequential manner as we grow in our understanding of God's Word and our connection to God through prayer, obedience, and faith. Willow Drive Baptist Church in Waco, Texas, has taken this model a step further by identifying some of the developmental tasks that occur during our transformation as believers:

Phase One—"Come & See"

This is the phase of spiritual infancy. The person has moved from being a non-believer to a convinced Christian. The key objective of this phase is centered around the salvation experience.

Phase Two—"Follow Me"

This is the phase of spiritual childhood. The disciple is becoming a laborer for Christ who is habitually and intentionally practicing the fundamentals of the Christlike walk and developing Christlike qualities. The key objectives of this phase include establishing the habits of the Christian life and becoming involved in ministry.

Phase Three—"Be With Me"

This is the phase of spiritual young adulthood. The disciple is now an equipped laborer. He has been trained and is actively involved in an ongoing ministry. The key objectives of this phase include initial involvement in some form of ministry and continuation of the spiritual growth process.

Phase Four—"Remain In Me"

This is the phase of spiritual parenthood. The disciple has become an experienced leader while still maintaining and deepening the character and ministry skills of the previous stages of discipleship. Some will advance to roles of leadership according to gifts, calling, and training. They will be equipping, leading, and guiding others in discipling ministries. The key objectives of this phase include reproducing other disciples and continuing on the path of spiritual growth.[4]

Reflect on these phases of growth in discipleship.

Establishing and Equipping

Too often, success in evangelism is seen as a verbal response by a non-Christian, indicating his or her personal support of a new set of convictions reflective of the Christian faith. The stress is on the verbal response. I surely do not want to sound as if I am not glad when one verbally testifies to becoming a Christian. In fact, there is great rejoicing in heaven when a sinner repents and accepts Jesus Christ as his or her personal Savior. But the goal of evangelism is not just to get a verbal response. The goal must also include helping the new believer to become established in the faith and equipped to serve Christ.

—Jim "Umfundisi" Lo

Our growth as disciples can be viewed in relation to our willingness to submit to God through our obedience to His commands, the disciplines of the Christian faith (taken from the Greek root mathetes, meaning pupil, learner, or apprentice). Listed below are some of the most basic skills:

- **My Attitude Toward God**

    Repent, then, and turn to God, so that your sins may be wiped out, that times of refreshing may come from the Lord. (Acts 3:19)

    1. Do I relate to God as the source of my forgiveness through His grace?
    2. Does my life demonstrate a love for Him and obedience to His commands?

- **My Attitude Toward People**

    Be devoted to one another in brotherly love. Honor one another above yourselves. (Romans 12:10)

1. How do I relate to other believers in Jesus Christ?

2. Am I showing God's love to those who do not yet know Jesus Christ?

3. Does my love demonstrate biblical perspectives (1 Corinthians 13)?

- **My Prayer Life**

   Do not be anxious about anything, but in everything, by prayer and petition, with thanksgiving, present your requests to God. And the peace of God, which transcends all understanding, will guard your hearts and your minds in Christ Jesus. (Philippians 4:6–7)

   1. How often am I praying? How much am I listening to God?

   2. In my prayers do I express my adoration for God, confess my sins, thank Him for the blessings He has placed in my life, and make my requests known?

- **My Time in God's Word**

   But the man who looks intently into the perfect law that gives freedom, and continues to do this, not forgetting what he has heard, but doing it—he will be blessed in what he does. (James 1:25)

   1. What is my plan for becoming more aware of God's Word?

   2. Am I memorizing Scripture?

   3. Do I take advantage of opportunities to gain new knowledge and insights regarding God's Word and its application to my life?

- **My Efforts to Share the Gospel**

   Therefore go and make disciples of all nations, baptizing

them in the name of the Father and of the Son and of the Holy Spirit, and teaching them to obey everything I have commanded you. (Matthew 28:19–20)

1. Do I look for opportunities to share the gospel with others?
2. Am I praying for these opportunities?

- **The Manner in Which I Use My Time, Effort, and Resources on God's Behalf**

  There are different kinds of gifts, but the same Spirit. There are different kinds of service, but the same Lord. There are different kinds of working, but the same God works all of them in all men. (1 Corinthians 12:4–6)

  1. Have I taken a spiritual gift inventory and identified my gifts?
  2. Do I look for opportunities to use my spiritual gifts on behalf of the gospel?

"Determining my Discipleship Quotient," an assessment tool designed to provide you with an opportunity to identify areas of strength and need in relation to discipleship, has been included in the "FAQ" section of this chapter. Take a few minutes now to assess your progress and growth as a disciple.

Connecting with Christ through Prayer

Discipleship means focusing on the "connection" disciplines of prayer and time in God's Word. One of the key cornerstones of a disciple's relationship with Jesus Christ is prayer. Through prayer we are granted the privilege of direct communication with the Creator of the universe. We are given the unbelievable opportunity to talk directly with God, sharing the burdens and joys of our lives. When we look at the life of Jesus, we can see that prayer played a central role in His life and in His relationship with God the Father. We will look at three separate strategies for prayer: The Hand Method, the Lord's Prayer, and the ACTS method.

The Hand Method

The Navigators have created a visual picture of prayer: an outstretched hand. Each of the fingers of the hand represents a recommended component of our conversations with God through prayer.

Praise: Voicing my wonder about who God is (Psalm 146:1–2)

Thanksgiving: Expressing my gratitude for what God has done for me (Ephesians 5:20)

Intercession: Praying for others (Ephesians 6:18–19)

Petition: Asking God for my needs (1 Samuel 1:27)

Confession: Agreeing with God about my sin (1 John 1:9)[5]

The Lord's Prayer

As the disciples traveled with Jesus, they observed Him as He regularly communicated with God through prayer. They observed the key role that this activity played in His life. As a result, they asked Jesus to teach them how to pray. Jesus responded with this model for prayer:

And when you pray, do not be like the hypocrites, for they love to pray standing in the synagogues and on the street corners to be seen by men. I tell you the truth, they have received their reward in full. But when you pray, go into your room, close the door and pray to your Father, who is unseen. Then your Father, who sees what is done in secret, will reward you. And when you pray, do not keep on babbling like pagans, for they think they will be heard because of their many words. Do not be like them, for your Father knows what you need before you ask him. This, then, is how you should pray:

Our Father in heaven, hallowed be your name, your kingdom come, your will be done on earth as it is in heaven. Give us today our daily bread. Forgive us our debts, as we also have forgiven our debtors. And lead us not into temptation, but deliver us from the evil one.

For if you forgive men when they sin against you, your heavenly Father will also forgive you. But if you do not forgive men their sins, your Father will not forgive your sins. (Matthew 6:5–15)

Bill Hybels is the pastor of Willow Creek Community Church in South Barrington, Illinois. In his book *Too Busy Not to Pray*, he provides the following analysis of Jesus' model prayer:

Besides praying privately and sincerely, Jesus counseled his disciples to pray specifically. He showed them what he meant by giving them a model prayer, the prayer we have all come to call the Lord's Prayer.

Jesus' prayer begins with the words **Our Father**. Never forget that you are God's child through Jesus Christ. You are praying to a Father who couldn't love you more than He already does.

The next phrase in the King James Version**, who art in heaven**, is a reminder that God is sovereign, majestic, and omnipotent. Nothing is too difficult for him. He is the mountain mover, He is bigger than any problem you could bring to him. Fix your eyes on his ability, not on your worth.

Hallowed be thy name. Don't let your prayers turn into a wish list for Santa Claus. Worship God and praise him when you come to him in prayer.

Thy kingdom come, thy will be done, on earth as it is in heaven. Submit your will to God's. Put his will first in your life—in your marriage, family, career, ministry, money, relationships, church.

Give us this day our daily bread. The Apostle Paul wrote, "In everything, by prayer and petition, with thanksgiving, present your request to God" (Phil. 4:6). Lay out all your concerns, whether big or small. If you need a miracle, ask for it without shrinking back.

Forgive us our debts, as we forgive our debtors. Be sure you're not the obstacle: confess your sins, receive forgiveness and begin to grow. Live with a forgiving spirit toward others. **Lead us not into temptation, but deliver us from evil.** Pray for protection from evil and victory over temptation.

For thine is the kingdom, the power, and the glory forever. End your prayer with more worship. Acknowledge that everything in heaven and earth is God's. Thank the Lord for caring about you, for making it possible for you to talk to him through prayer.

Amen. Let it be so.[6]

The ACTS Method

The ACTS Method is an acronym for **A**doration, **C**onfession, **T**hanksgiving, and **S**upplication. Although the exact source of this method is unknown, it has become a popular and effective method for prayer. Many of us tend to focus on thanking God and sharing our list of needs. These are important components of prayer, but we also need to spend time with God confessing our sins and praising Him for His awesome glory and magnificence. The ACTS method provides a means for thinking about the varied components of prayer. The following is a description of the ACTS method developed by the Navigators:

Adoration is proclaiming and exalting God's name, attributes, and character.

Let everything that has breath praise the LORD. Praise the LORD. (Psalm 150:6)

Confession is agreeing with and acknowledging your failures to meet and comply with God's standard of perfection.

He who conceals his sins does not prosper, but whoever confesses and renounces them finds mercy. (Proverbs 28:13)

Thanksgiving is recognizing and recounting God's gracious acts and influences both in and around your life.

Give thanks to the Lord, for he is good. His love endures forever. (Psalm 136:1)

Supplication is God's people invoking God's power to accomplish God's purpose.

*Until now you have not asked for anything in my name. Ask
and you will receive, and your joy will be complete.* (John
16:24)[7]

Connecting with Christ through His Word

As we have emphasized throughout this text, God's Word is the
ultimate source of wisdom and guidance. It is the inspired message
from God to His people. If we desire to follow God's commands, live
in a manner that will be pleasing to Him, know of His promises, catch
a glimpse of His magnificence, learn of His ongoing role in the history
of the universe—we must take the time and effort to read the Bible.

One strategy for getting acquainted with your Bible is to engage
in a scheduled "Quiet Time" with God. This too requires
discipline—scheduling a specific time every day to get away from
your busy schedule for the purposes of praying and studying God's
Word. Once you have made that commitment, here is one approach
to systematically making the most of your time with God:

- Start with prayer. Ask God to prepare you to meet with
  Him. If there is something in your life that you know
  displeases Him, confess it. Let Him forgive you so that
  nothing will hinder your communion together.

- Read a specific passage of Scripture—perhaps a chapter or
  two. If you are not very familiar with the Bible, you may
  wish to start with the New Testament. Many people think
  that the Gospel of John is a good place to start. Perhaps you
  would enjoy reading one or two of the Psalms every day.

- Meditate on the passage for a while after you have read
  it. Think about what you read, and ask yourself what it
  means. What does God want you to do? Remember, even
  though you may not understand all you read in the Bible,
  you can still obey what you do understand.

- Write down questions about the passage as you read. It is
  good to write down the things you learn and the questions
  you have. Later you can search out the answers from
  someone who knows the subject or from Bible commentaries.

- Then read the passage again. Reading it a second time usually brings to light things you didn't notice the first time. This is a great way to learn on your own, for as you read, you'll have God's Holy Spirit as your teacher (John 14:26).

- Finally, pray again. Thank God for sending His Son to die for you. Thank Him for giving you His Word (the Bible) because without it you would have no answers to life's big questions. Thank Him for teaching you from the passage you have just read.[8]

As a final strategy for interacting with God's Word, consider the "Timothy Method"[9] based upon the following Scripture:

All Scripture is God-breathed and is useful for teaching, rebuking, correcting and training in righteousness. (2 Timothy 3:16)

Application of the Timothy Method involves following a specific sequence of questions as you study God's Word:

- **Reading** the portion of Scripture that you have selected.

- **Teaching**: Ask yourself, "What does this passage teach?"

- **Rebuking:** Ask yourself, "Am I falling short in this area? If so, how?"

- **Correcting:** Ask yourself, "What is the opposite of my sin?" (e.g., the opposite of anger may be self-control)

- **Training:** Ask yourself, "What do I need to do to stay on track?"

On Following

The concept of discipleship is an uncommon one in today's society, but in Jesus' time the idea was as familiar as bread, rocks, or air. Disciples were young people who followed their mentor—specifically, their *rabbi*—around to learn his viewpoint, his practices, his take on God and the world. The disciple's ultimate goal was to become more and more like his rabbi until eventually he could think and behave just as the rabbi would think or behave. There were little pockets of disciples everywhere, and Jesus' twelve disciples were the ones who made up His particular group of followers, literally because they followed Him around in everything, from the mundane to the water-into-wine spectacular.

I often wish that I could have the chance to follow Jesus around a bit, to get to know the slump of His shoulders, to learn the tone of His voice when He was especially happy. I wish that I could know how He would respond when provoked or what He would say when taken off guard. I often tell myself that it would be easier for me to be a Christian if I could walk around with Jesus for a while. Then, certainly, I would know Christ and Christianity much better, wouldn't I?

Well, probably not. Although I don't have the option to walk step by step behind my Rabbi, I have plenty of ways to connect with Him. I can read about Him in the Bible and I can follow others who seek to know Him. I can talk to Him daily, and if I learn to listen well, I can hear Him speaking back to me. I can't attend weddings or eat lunch with Him, but I can know Him. The decade of my birth has nothing to do with my ability to follow. If I really want to, I can still be a disciple. The option is always open; I simply must do the work of following.

—Lisa Velthouse

FAQ

Q. I have tried several times to increase the amount of time that I pray and spend in God's Word, but I always fall short. What do you suggest?

A. We know that this is a challenge. For all of us, with our busy schedules and the distractions of daily life, it is sometimes hard to get into the practice of meeting with God every day. It takes approximately three weeks for you to become familiar with a new task and it takes another three weeks to become comfortable with a new habit. Again we learn that discipleship is a process, not an event.

One good place to start is by scheduling a specific time in your planner or PDA. So, for example, every morning or every evening, you have a scheduled time to meet with God. Just like you make exercise or other activities part of your daily regimen, you include time to meet with God.

Another good strategy is to find an accountability partner who will either join you for prayer and Bible study on a regular basis, or who will serve to check on your progress by asking, "How's it going with your quiet time?"

 Reaction and Reflection

Determining My Discipleship Quotient

On a scale of one to ten, rate your "discipleship quotient" in the following areas:

My Attitude toward God

Repent, then, and turn to God, so that your sins may be wiped out, that times of refreshing may come from the Lord. (Acts 3:19)

Repentant   **Rebellious**

   10   9   8   7   6   5   4   3   2   1

My Attitude toward People

Be devoted to one another in brotherly love. Honor one another above yourselves. (Romans 12:10)

Relational									**Reclusive**
10	9	8	7	6	5	4	3	2	1

My Prayer Life

Do not be anxious about anything, but in everything, by prayer and petition, with thanksgiving, present your requests to God. And the peace of God, which transcends all understanding, will guard your hearts and your minds in Christ Jesus. (Philippians 4:6–7)

Reflective									**Ritualistic**
10	9	8	7	6	5	4	3	2	1

My Time in God's Word

But the man who looks intently into the perfect law that gives freedom, and continues to do this, not forgetting what he has heard, but doing it—he will be blessed in what he does. (James 1:25)

Regular									**Reluctant**
10	9	8	7	6	5	4	3	2	1

My Efforts to Share the Gospel

Therefore go and make disciples of all nations, baptizing them in the name of the Father and of the Son and of the Holy Spirit, and teaching them to obey everything I have commanded you. (Matthew 28:19–20)

Reaching									**Resting**
10	9	8	7	6	5	4	3	2	1

The Manner in Which I Use My Time, Effort, and Resources on God's Behalf

There are different kinds of gifts, but the same Spirit. There are different kinds of service, but the same Lord. There are different kinds of working, but the same God works all of them in all men. (1 Corinthians 12:4-6)

Radical   **Reasonable**
  10   9   8   7   6   5   4   3   2   1

What did you learn about yourself?

What are some areas of strength in your spiritual life as a disciple?

What are some areas that may need some additional effort?

A Ministry Memory

The J.C. Body Shop

Not far from my office on the Indiana Wesleyan University campus is a new, artistically styled building called the *J. C. Body Shop*. A few friends and I were privileged to found that organization in 1981 with about ten teens and a makeshift meeting space. Since then, thousands have gone through the program. Although it sounds rather simplistic, the cornerstone is discipleship. From the initial planning meeting through those first key years, only those who had been through a discipleship program could lead. Likewise, those who led were to disciple others. Little did I know when I left to pursue doctoral studies at Miami University (1985) what the future would hold. The remarkable ramifications of discipleship would lead to solid spiritual *and* cement foundations.

Fifteen years later, I returned to the same campus. Now my own four sons benefit from this youth ministry and the mentoring of a host of new leaders. You just might think that discipleship is the perfect way to grow and sustain a ministry. It is. As this chapter hopefully has pointed out—it's God-ordained.

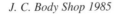

J. C. Body Shop 1985   *J.C. Body Shop 2003*

Suggested Readings and Resources

Blackaby, H. T., and Claude V. King. *Experiencing God: Knowing and Doing the Will of God.* Nashville: LifeWay Press, 1990.

Curtis, B., and John Eldredge. *The Sacred Romance: Drawing Close to the Heart of God.* Nashville: Thomas Nelson, 1997.

Curtis, B., and John Eldredge. *The Sacred Romance: Drawing Close to the Heart of God Workbook.* Nashville: Thomas Nelson, 1997.

Garner, J. Bradley. *Adventures in Discipleship: An Interactive Study in the Gospel of Mark.* Kent, OH: Riverwood Community Chapel, 2000.

Hybels, B., and Lavonne Neff. *Too Busy Not to Pray: Slowing Down to Be With God.* Downers Grove, IL: InterVarsity Press, 1998.

Laurie, G. *Discipleship: The Next Step in Following Jesus.* Boulder, CO: Harvest House, 1998.

Navigators. *Growing in Discipleship.* Colorado Springs: NavPress Publishing Group, 1973.

Peterson, E. H. *A Long Obedience in the Same Direction: Discipleship in an Instant Society.* Rev. ed. Downers Grove, IL: InterVarsity Press, 2000.

Endnotes

1. Original source unknown. Tim Hansel, Eating Problems for Breakfast (Nashville: Word Publishing|Thomas Nelson, 1988), 94-195. Available online at http://www.bible.org/illus.php?topic_id=413 (accessed August 9, 2007), http://www.nilacharal.com/news/religion/chris6.html (accessed August 9, 2007), and http://www.sermonillustrations.com/a-z/d/disciples.htm (accessed August 9, 2007). For related issues see Klyne Snodgrass, Between Two Truths - Living with Biblical Tensions (Grand Rapids: Zondervan Publishing House, 1990) and Nicholas Mokelke, Bits and Pieces (September 19, 1991): 2.

2. "Make Disciples, Not Just Converts: Evangelism without Discipleship Dispenses Cheap Grace," *Christianity Today* 43 (October 25, 1999), 48.

3. Rick Warren, *The Purpose-Driven Church* (Grand Rapids, MI: Zondervan, 1995). As presented by Willow Drive Baptist Church available online at http://www.wdbc.net (accessed August 6, 2007).

4. Ibid.

5. "The Hand Method" for prayer was developed by the Navigators. Information regarding this approach to prayer (and the descriptions cited) available online at http://www.navigators.org (accessed August 7, 2007).

6. Bill Hybels, *Too Busy Not to Pray* (Downers Grove, IL: InterVarsity Press, 1988), 45-46.

7. The original source for the ACTS method is unknown.

8. A six-step plan for extablishing a quiet time. Available online at http://www.backtothebible.org/knowGod/step3.htm.

9. The original source of the Timothy method is unknown.

conclusion

Yet for us there is but one God, the Father, from whom all things came and for whom we live; and there is but one Lord, Jesus Christ, through whom all things came and through whom we live.
(1 Corinthians 8:6)

conclusion

When a good book ends, sometimes a reader sighs, closes it, and savors the story a bit longer. Some books end too quickly. The characters become friends whose lives are confined to the pages between the book's covers. Some books have brilliant lessons or storylines that will inform discussions for a lifetime. In nearly all of these cases, the readers don't reopen their books, but instead discuss them from memory.

If we have done our work well, *Straight Talk* will be different. It's intended to be a reference work—a tool for many discussions and questions, a book to be reopened on many occasions.

Years from now, when my personal stories are a bit dated, the key doctrines represented in this text will still be current. The Scriptures and their application are solid for all generations.

In the closing section of chapter 8, the story of the *J. C. Body Shop* is proof of the timeless truths contained in the Scriptures. The teens that attend today may find many of the stories from the early 1980s difficult to understand, or difficult to apply to today's issues. However, these same teens can relate to the foundational teachings—the key doctrines—even if presented in the wrappings of the early '80s. The same can be said of churches through the ages, whether they are English churches with foundations dug in the

Middle Ages or churches transplanted to another continent. The main doctrines of today's Christianity are the same as those of the early church and are based on the same Scriptures.

Throughout *Straight Talk*, you have been asked to look at several Scriptures—the actual basis for the doctrines of Christianity. Perhaps the text has helped you to realize that some of the information behind your religious decisions has been misleading or, at the least, incomplete. Or, perhaps *Straight Talk* has helped you understand more clearly the true story about Christ and the foundation of Christianity.

In the preface of this book, I tell the story of my first encounter with a famous professor, and how little I knew about Christianity in 1975:

> Trying to disguise my nervousness, I pointed to the oversized historic portrait behind the large worn wooden desk of Dr. Wilbur Williams and said conversationally, "That's a great picture. Is that your great-grandmother?"

> He looked up at me and, for a moment, time stood still. In a voice that echoed through the halls of the gloomy basement into the shadowed corridors of the distant past, a voice undoubtedly borrowed from God, he replied, "That, young man, is John Wesley."

A bit later in the preface, I challenge you with the following:

> Imagine yourself sitting at that large worn wooden desk. Instead of an oversized historic portrait of Wesley, a picture of Jesus Christ hangs behind you on the wall. How would you answer if one of your friends walked into the room and asked, "Who is that?" How would you respond if your friend's next question was, "Why do you have it in your office?" What if your friend asked, "Can you tell me in a nutshell what He believed?" Could you do that?

Now that you've finished this text, let's return to these same questions, but change the context a bit.

Imagine years from now walking into an ultramodern futuristic office in a tall building that houses a leading technology firm. The office is rather stark, featuring a trendy sleek desk, a few keepsakes nearly hidden on a small space-age brushed titanium stand in the far corner, and one mauve and yellow metal flower arrangement—a suspended hologram above the desk's corner.

The wall behind the desk doesn't display an antiquated oversized picture of Jesus. Instead, you see a plasma screen with multiple images of Christ from various movies. The silent scenes range from Mel Gibson's *The Passion of the Christ* to Mel Brooke's outtakes. Random still shots from familiar paintings drift across the screen. Modern images and cartoon figures of Christ flash in random order. Even Chaim Potok's Picasso-style crucifixion painting appears.

You don't need to ask, "Who's that?" or "What did He believe?" You realize that the context might have changed, but not the content. The Jesus behind those artists' interpretations of Christ is the same Jesus behind lessons studied in the J. C. Body Shop, those studied in the basement of the old church building, and those memorized in the remote fourth-century monasteries of Egyptian deserts. The Scriptures presented in *Straight Talk* form the basic doctrines of orthodox Christianity and, hopefully, have helped you to see the real Jesus.

Culture and context will continue to change, but the basic Christian doctrines will remain unchanged.

appendix a
helpful scripture references

When you are in danger or have the blues . . Psalm 34; Psalm 91; Luke 8:22–25

When discouraged...................... Isaiah 40; 1 Corinthians 10:13

When God seems distant................................. Psalm 139

When doubts come .... John 7:17

When you feel down and out .... Romans 8:31–39

If faith needs stirring .... Hebrews 11

When you forget your blessings .... Psalm 103

If you want to be fruitful................................... John 15

For Paul's rules on how to get along with others .... Romans 12

For Paul's secret for happiness..................... Colossians 3:12–17

When you think of investments and returns............... Mark 10:17–31

For a great invitation and a great opportunity.................. Isaiah 55

When lonely or fearful .... Psalm 23

When you want rest and peace..................... Matthew 11:25–30

For Jesus' idea of prayer .... Luke 11:1–13

When your prayers grow narrow or selfish .... Psalm 67

For James' idea of religion .... James 1:19–27

For the prophet's idea of religion .... Isaiah 1:10–18; Micah 6:6–8

When you are sick .... James 5:13–16; Psalm 41

When you have sinned .... Psalm 51; 1 John 1:8–9; Hebrews 7:25

When in sorrow .... John 14; Psalm 46

When you travel....................................... Psalm 121

When you worry .... Matthew 6:19–34

For the prophets' picture of worship that counts............. Isaiah 58:1–12

For assurance...................................... Romans 8:1–30

When you grow bitter or critical....................... 1 Corinthians 13

For courage for your task.................. Joshua 1; 2 Corinthians 12:9

For Jesus' definition of a Christian . . John 3:16; Matthew 10:32–33, 22:35–40, 25:31–46

For Paul's idea of Christianity .... 2 Corinthians 5:15–19

Before church service .... Psalm 84

appendix b
scriptures by topic

Doctrine
Matthew 5:8
Matthew 6:21
Acts 1:24
Acts 15:8
Romans 3:21–26
Romans 5:1–3
Romans 8:31–34
Romans 10:4–13
1 Corinthians 8:6
1 Corinthians 12:13
1 Timothy 2:5–6
1 Timothy 4:6
1 Timothy 6:20–21
2 Timothy 3:16
2 Timothy 4:3
Hebrews 4:12–13

Salvation
Matthew 1:21
John 19:28
Acts 3:18
Romans 16:25
1 Corinthians 1:18
1 Corinthians 15:3–6
Titus 3:3
Hebrews 2:3
James 1:21
2 Peter 3:9

Serving Christ
Psalm 27:14
Psalm 32:8
Proverbs 3:5–6
Proverbs 11:14; 12:15
Ecclesiastes 11:4
Matthew 6:10, 26, 34
Matthew 8:34–35

John 3:34
John 6:40
John 15:4
Acts 6:2
Hebrews 1:14
Hebrews 7:17

Sanctification
Acts 16:27
1 Corinthians 1:2
2 Corinthians 1:21
2 Thessalonians 2:13
Ephesians 3:19
Hebrews 10:10

Evangelism
Matthew 22:9
John 12:15–17
Acts 1:21
Acts 9:15
1 Corinthians 9:16–17
2 Corinthians 4:1–5
Ephesians 3:8–10
1 Thessalonians 2:4–12
1 Timothy 6:3–21

Sexual Purity
Ecclesiastes 8:15
Isaiah 1:18
Matthew 26:21
Romans 8:8
1 Corinthians 7:1
Galatians 5:24
Ephesians 1:3–5
Ephesians 5:3, 25
2 Timothy 2:21
1 John 2:16

appendix c
insights from a religion professor

Lists like the one on the opposite page should come with a warning:

Caution. This list can be hazardous
to your spiritual health.

They're dangerous because they can fool you into thinking of the Bible as just a book of advice. Got a problem? Find the passage that tells you what to do. "I need to know about 'sexual purity,' so I'll read Galatians 5:24."

The Bible is full of good counsel, but wasn't meant to be read as an anthology of advice. God is not "Dear Abby." The Bible is the story of God's plan to save the world. So, read it like a story, understanding each verse in context, seeking to learn all you can about the Lord and His work in the world.

I *have* found lists like this to be very helpful when used correctly. When I vaguely remember a passage but wonder what it actually says or where to find it, or when I'm studying a topic in one passage and wonder what else the Bible has to say about it, such lists can save a ton of time.

Use such lists often; just don't let them be the only way you read the Bible. Instead, slowly and carefully get to know who God is and what He is doing. More than fatherly advice, you'll get to know your heavenly Father. More than helpful tips, you'll learn how to help Him change the world.

—Dr. Steve Lennox

glossary of
christian
terminology

Do your best to present yourself to God as one approved,
a workman who does not need to be ashamed and who
correctly handles the word of truth.
(2 Timothy 2:15)

glossary of
Christian terminology

The following definitions represent their respective terms' use within the context of Christianity. They also are written from a Christian perspective. Some terms are best understood through word studies (i.e., uncovering a term's origins and root meanings as used in the Old Testament [OT] and New Testament [NT]). The primary languages of the Old and New Testaments are Hebrew and Koine Greek, respectively. Also, where appropriate, reference and bibliographic entries (Bibl) are given. For more information, see *The New Bible Dictionary* (Tyndale House, 1982) and *The New International Dictionary of the Christian Church* (Zondervan Publishing, 1974). For a more in-depth treatment of subjects, see *The New International Standard Bible Encyclopedia* (ISBE), (William B. Eerdmans, 1982). The most thorough Bible* dictionary is a six-volume set by Doubleday Press, *The Anchor Bible Dictionary* (1992).

*denotes a glossary term

adultery: unfaithfulness in a marriage relationship; when a marriage partner voluntarily has sex with someone other than his or her spouse; a sin listed in numerous biblical passages, and included in the Ten Commandments (Exodus 20:1–17, 32:15–16); any immoral act such as adultery runs contrary to the basic teachings of Christ* (Matthew 5–7, 19; Romans 1; James 1; Titus 2). The high moral standards of the early Christians factored greatly in the appeal and growth of Christianity*, an observation made even by renowned scholars generally opposed to Christianity*. William Lecky, a British adversary of organized Christianity*, admitted this:

It was reserved for Christianity to present to the world an ideal character which through all the changes of eighteen centuries has inspired the hearts of men with an impassioned love; has shown itself capable of acting on all ages, nations, temperaments and conditions; has been not only the highest pattern of virtue, but the strongest incentive to its practice. The simple record of these three short years of active life [Christ's last three] has done more to regenerate and soften mankind than all the disquisitions of philosophers and all the exhortations of moralists" (*History of European Morals from Augustus to Charlemagne* [New York: D. Appleton and Co., 1903], 8).

In his classic, *The Decline and Fall of the Roman Empire*, Edward Gibbon (a humanist, d. 1794), conceded that in addition to the "obvious" success and popularity of the Christian doctrine* itself, there were five "secondary causes" that factored in the Christian faith's "remarkable victory over the established religions of the earth," with one cause being:

IV. THE PURE AND AUSTERE MORALS OF THE CHRISTIANS. But the primitive Christian demonstrated his faith by his virtues; and it was very justly supposed that the divine persuasion which enlightened or subdued the understanding must at the same time purify the heart and direct the actions of the believer . . . shall slightly mention two motives . . . repentance for their past sins and the laudable desire of supporting the reputation of the society in which they were engaged (in *The Portable Gibbon: The Decline and Fall of the Roman Empire*, Dero A. Saunders, ed. [New York: Viking Press, 1952], 284–285).

agnostic: (from Greek *a* + *gnosis*, without knowledge); a person who neither accepts nor rejects the existence of God, claiming that empirical evidence on such a matter is impossible to attain; most agnostics develop a naturalistic* worldview* that rejects belief in the Trinity or the divinity of Christ*; however, many agnostics endeavor to develop their morality and ethics upon Christian principles.

Antichrist: a great antagonist who will rise up shortly before Christ's* "second coming*"' (1 John 4:1–3); the Antichrist will oppose Christ* and His followers and fill the world with wickedness; ultimately, the Antichrist will suffer defeat by the Christian forces at the Battle of Armageddon and be eternally damned to the lake of fire—already prepared for Satan* and his followers (Matthew 25:41); along with Satan*, the beast [Antichrist] will be "thrown into the lake of burning sulfur . . . [and] they will be tormented night and day for ever and ever" (Revelation 20:10); although he is never given this title, most scholars identify the False Prophet with the Beast of Revelation 13–20, who will appear at the end of human history.

antichrist: one who opposes Christ* (1 John 2:22); a false Messiah (1 John 2:18; 2 John 1:7).

Apocrypha: (neuter plural of Greek adjective *apokryphos,* hidden, concealed) early Jewish writings that Protestantism* dubbed as noncanonical because they were never published in connection with the canonical Scriptures; there is no evidence that God inspired the writing of these texts, and none of these works is cited in the book of Revelation, whereas many canonical books are; although most of these texts are of dubious authenticity, they are nevertheless valued for private study—books to be "hidden away" and not read in public; at the Council of Trent (1546) and again at the First Vatican Council (1869–70) the Roman Catholic Church* embraced the Apocrypha as biblical canon*, which accounts for the extra books in a Catholic Bible* (compared with that of most Protestant Bibles*); the Apocryphal books contained in English Bibles* appear in the following order: (1) 1 Esdras; (2) 2 Esdras; (3) Tobit; (4) Judith; (5) Additions to the Book of Esther; (6) Wisdom of Solomon; (7) Ecclesiasticus (Sirach); (8) Baruch, including the letter of Jeremiah; (9) Song of the Three Young Men; (10) Susanna; (11) Bel and the Dragon; (12) Prayer of Manasseh; (13) 1 Maccabees; (14) 2 Maccabees; the Roman Catholic Apocrypha ("Deuterocanonical Books") do not include 1 & 2 Esdras and the Prayer of Manasseh; works not included in the list of fourteen are generally referred to as part of the pseudepigrapha; the editors of the scholarly Anchor Bible series differ with the traditional definition of "Apocrypha" and assert:

> An apocryphon is literally a hidden writing, kept secret for the initiate and too exalted for the general public; virtually none of these books makes such a pretense . . . Leaving aside the question of canonicity, Christians and Jews now unite in recognizing the importance of these books for tracing the history of Judaism and Jewish thought in the centuries between the last of the Hebrew Scriptures and the advent of Christianity (*The Anchor Bible Series*, 42 vols., William F. Albright and David N. Freedman, gen. eds. [Garden City, NY: Doubleday & Co., 1964–?], viii).

Bibl: Bruce M. Metzger, *An Introduction to the Apocrypha* (New York: Oxford University Press, 1957); for the Catholic decision on the Apocrypha see 5–7, 189–204; Roger Beckwith, *The Old Testament Canon of the New Testament Church* (Grand Rapids, MI: Wm. B. Eerdmans Publishing Co., 1986); Floyd V. Filson, *Which Books Belong in the Bible?* (Philadelphia: Westminster Press, 1957); James H. Charlesworth, ed., *The Old Testament Pseudepigrapha*, 2 vols. (Garden City, NY: Doubleday & Co., 1985).

apologetics: Presenting the claims for Christianity* to those who are skeptical by using reason, scientific findings, and the presuppositions of other worldviews as a starting point for discussion. It is often contrasted with "dogmatics," a presentation of Christianity* that starts with Scripture, church tradition, and the assumptions of those who already believe in making its case. Josh McDowell is probably the foremost Christian apologist in the academic world today. Other well-known Christian apologists include C. S. Lewis and Francis Schaeffer.

Bibl: Josh McDowell, *The New Evidence That Demands a Verdict* (Nashville: Nelson Reference, 1999).

apostle: (from Greek verb *apostello,* to send with a purpose) one sent on a mission (2 Corinthians 8:23; Philippians 2:25); often used in reference to "the Apostles," (an authoritative group of twelve men Christ* chose for special instruction and intensive training and who were commissioned to spread His teachings [Acts 1:8]); St. Paul*, although not among the original twelve, is also referred to as an apostle; the twelve apostles are listed in Mark 3:16 19:

Simon (to whom he gave the name Peter); James son of Zebedee and his brother John (to them he gave the name Boanerges, which means Sons of Thunder); Andrew, Philip, Bartholomew, Matthew, Thomas, James son of Alphaeus, Thaddaeus, Simon the Zealot and Judas Iscariot, who betrayed him.

Matthias replaced Judas Iscariot (Acts 1:26).

Bibl: Donald Guthrie, *The Apostles* (Grand Rapids, MI: Zondervan Corp., 1975); Alexander B. Bruce, *The Training of the Twelve* (Grand Rapids, MI: Kregel Publications, 1971); W. M. Ramsay, *St. Paul the Traveller and the Roman Citizen* (Grand Rapids, MI: Baker Book House, 1962).

Apostles' Creed: Perhaps the earlist summative statement that includes the key doctrines of the Christian faith. By AD 100, the church had a serious battle with heresies*, such as the Gnostics, and the creed was used as a standard to measure orthodoxy. At first, it likely was a formula and often used to answer key questions during rituals, such as baptism. By AD 150, the formula had certainly become a creed—as evident in an ancient Roman text. We find in the New Testament* that heresies* were already springing up (e.g., 1 Timothy 2:5–6; 3:16; 6:20), and a clear undersanding of orthodox* teaching was imperative. Various writers in the Middle Ages mention the Apostles' Creed, attributing its origin to the early church. Many denominations*, such as the Reformed Church, adhere to it today. Some scholars list the twelve apostles among its authors. Around AD 400, St. Ambrose (the Bishop of Milan, Italy, instrumental in the conversion of St. Augustine) preached that the creed showed evidence of being arranged "by twelve separate workmen." His contemporary, Rufinus, concurs with the apostolic authorship and gives a thorough explanation in his account. He also endorses a popular notion that its origin is traced to the Day of Pentecost, and that the apostles formed it there while waiting for the Holy Spirit*. A detailed discussion of the creed can be found on the *Catholic Encyclopedia's* Web site, referenced below.

Catholic Encyclopedia, S.V. "Apostles' Creed": http://www.new advent.org/cathen/01629a.htm (accessed August 6, 2007)

Bibl: Paul T. Fuhrmann, *An Introduction to the Great Creeds of the Church* (Philadelphia: The Westminster Press, 1960), 19–33.

atheism: (from Greek *a* + *theos,* without God): a belief system that assumes a naturalistic* worldview* and rejects the reality of any supernatural being; communism, as espoused by Karl Marx, was atheistic in its claim that physical matter (materialism) was all that existed; in recent years, Madelyn Murray O'Hair was the most outspoken advocate for atheism in American culture and politics.

atonement: a divine transaction whereby sinful human beings are brought into a right relationship with God through the death of His Son, Jesus Christ*; in the Old Testament*, this right relationship was attained through a blood sacrifice, a foreshadowing of Christ's* redemption on the cross; various theories have been proposed through the centuries as to how we are reconciled to God through the death of His Son; the fact of such redemption is clearly stated in the New Testament* (2 Corinthians 5:17–23), but the particular means whereby this relationship is restored is not given; the majority of Christians hold to the "substitution" theory which proposes that Jesus died in the place of condemned humanity, thus appeasing the wrath of God and purchasing our salvation through His blood.

Bibl: D. M. Baille, *God Was in Christ* (New York: Charles Scribner's Sons, 1955); Jurgan Moltmann, *The Crucified God* (New York: Doubleday, 1978).

backsliding: (slang) a lapse in one's spiritual status, a reverting to sinful ways after the conversion experience; Protestantism* is sharply divided over the issue of how far one can "backslide" after conversion, more specifically, whether one can lose his or her salvation; the camps are polarized around the teachings of two men, John Calvin (1509–1564), who asserted that it is impossible to lose one's salvation, a doctrine* commonly referred to as "eternal security"*, and Jacob Arminius (1560–1609), who argued that it is possible for Christians to fall from grace*; the two doctrinal camps are known as Calvinism and Arminianism, with many more doctrinal differences than the above; see salvation* and sin*.

Bible: (from Greek *biblion,* book, taken from Byblos, the ancient Phoenician city known for papyrus exports) a collection of books recognized by Christians as the inspired word of God, written by man, and which should not be altered (Matthew 5:17–19; Revelation 20:18–19); the Old Testament* canon* was closed by 100 BC; Moses wrote the first five books (the Pentateuch) sometime between 1420 BC and 1270 BC, thus beginning the written stage of God's Word (and the biblical canon*), and Hebrew prophets and key personalities would write the rest of the OT books; for the New Testament, the earliest known mention of a definite list of Scriptures (canon*) was in AD 120, and the Church Council of Carthage (AD 397 or 419) was the first formal action of ratifying an established canon* by the bishops of the entire Christian Church. Since the earliest stages of Christianity*, groups have severely distorted the content of the original Scriptures, claiming new revelations and written works to be canonized—such claims are inconsistent with the true Scriptures, (e.g., Gnosticism in antiquity and Mormonism in the nineteenth century); see cults*.

Bibl: Samuel J. Schultz, *The Old Testament Speaks* (San Francisco: Harper & Row, 1960); Peter C. Craige, *The Old Testament: Its*

Background, Growth, and Contents (Nashville: Abingdon, 1986); Victor R. Hamilton, *Handbook on the Pentateuch* (Grand Rapids, MI: Baker, 1982); Robert H. Gundry, *A Survey of the New Testament* (Grand Rapids, MI: Zondervan Corp., 1970); Merrill C. Tenney, *New Testament Survey* (Grand Rapids, MI: Wm. B. Eerdmans Pub. Co., 1961); John Drane, *Introducing the New Testament* (San Francisco: Harper and Row, 1986); David Alexander and Pat Alexander, *Eerdmans' Handbook to the Bible* (Oxford: Eerdmans Pub., 1973); Gleason Archer, A *Survey of the Old Testament* (Chicago: Moody Press, 1964); F. F. Bruce, *The Books and the Parchments*, rev. ed. (Westwood: Fleming H. Revell Co., 1963); and *The New Testament Documents, Are They Reliable?* (Downers Grove, IL: InterVarsity Press, 1964); Ralph Earle, *How We Got Our Bible* (Grand Rapids, MI: Baker Book House, 1971); Norman L. Geisler and William E. Nix, *A General Introduction to the Bible* (Chicago: Moody Press, 1968); Bruce M. Metzger, *The Text of the New Testament* (New York: Oxford University Press, 1968).

Bible commentaries: books with the main purpose of offering a systematic series of explanations for the biblical text; e.g., a popular and well-regarded commentary series for the New Testament is William Barclay's *Daily Bible Series*, rev. ed. (Philadelphia: Westminster Press, 1975–1976); for a complete list of reputable commentaries for each of the biblical books, see "The Evaluation and Use of Commentaries" in Gordon D. Fee and Douglas Stuart, *How to Read the Bible for All Its Worth* (Grand Rapids, MI: Zondervan Press, 1982), 219–224; Fee and Stuart assert: "What you want a commentary for is basically to supply three things: (1) helps on sources and information about the historical context, (2) answers to those manifold content questions, and (3) thorough discussions of difficult texts as to the possibilities of meaning with supporting arguments" (p. 219).

Bibl: Fee and Stuart, *How to Read the Bible*, 219–224; "Concordances, Dictionaries and Atlases" in R. C. Sproul's *Knowing Scripture* (Downers Grove, IL: InterVarsity Press, 1977), 119–120; F. F. Bruce, ed., *The New International Commentary on the New Testament* (Grand Rapids, MI: William B. Eerdmans Publishing Co., 1971).

canon: (from Greek *kanon,* reed, from which measuring rulers came, thus, the later meaning "standard") a standard; the authoritative list of books decreed by early church councils to be Holy Scriptures; Protestants* generally adhere to the strict OT* Hebrew canon and the NT* canon, for a total of sixty-six canonical books; the early church and its Councils used three criteria for establishing canonicity: (1) attribution to apostles* or their close associates (all living during the first century AD), (2) ecclesiastical recognition—usage by leading churches and/or by a majority of churches, and (3) congruence with sound doctrine* and standards consistent with known apostolic witness; perhaps as early as AD 80, and certainly by the late fourth century AD (at the Council of Carthage) a fixed canon was in place.

Bibl: F. F. Bruce, *The Books and the Parchments,* rev. ed. (Westwood: Fleming H. Revell Co., 1963); and *The New Testament Documents: Are They Reliable?* (Downers Grove, IL: InterVarsity Press, 1964); Norman L. Geisler and William E. Nix, *A General Introduction to the Bible* (Chicago: Moody Press, 1968); Ralph Earle, *How We Got Our Bible* (Grand Rapids, MI: Baker Book House, 1971); Bruce M. Metzger, *The Text of the New Testament* (New York: Oxford University Press, 1968); John Warwick Montgomery, *History and Christianity* (Downers Grove, IL: InterVarsity Press, 1964); Michael J. Wilkins and J. P. Moreland, *Jesus Under Fire* (Grand Rapids, MI: Zondervan, 1995).

catholic: (from Greek *kata holikos,* according to the whole, universal) used in reference to the undivided and universal Christian Church; in the Apostles' Creed* the word "catholic" means "universal" and not the Roman Catholic Church*; e.g., "I believe in the Holy Ghost; the holy catholic church . . ." (ca. AD 150).

Catholic Church, specifically Roman Catholic Church: a religious institution claiming historical continuity with the ancient Christian Church; the Catholic Church's integrity rests "on the unity of the episcopate centered on its Petrine origin at Rome"; i.e., the papal succession is traced to St. Peter, one of Jesus' twelve disciples*; St. Peter, according to a very strong tradition, was buried in Rome at the site now occupied by the Vatican—papal headquarters of the Catholic Church," (W. H. C. Frend, *The Rise of Christianity* [Philadelphia: Fortress Press, 1984], 324); the claim of supremacy for the bishop of Rome (pope) was challenged by other bishops. Eventually this led to a split (schism) in Christendom*— those rejecting papal authority forming the various branches of the Orthodox Church, and those holding to the supremacy of the pope forming the Roman Catholic Church; the final break between these two branches of Christendom* occurred in 1054 when the bishops of Rome and Constantinople both excommunicated the other; although the Catholic claim to a Petrine succession appears historically correct, the importance of such a succession is suspect; a more important issue is the Catholic Church's doctrine* of salvation*, which contradicts that recorded in the Scriptures and held by the early church; thus, the Protestants*, led by Martin Luther in the early sixteenth century, officially broke from their parent religious organization, the Roman Catholic Church, forming the third great branch of Christianity*. One should consult the various new "official" documents on the Catholic-Lutheran Accord, May 1999, for an understanding of the significant shift toward reconciliation between Roman Catholics and Protestants* (cf. official Catholic and Lutheran Web sites).

Bibl: Kenneth Scott Latourette, *A History of Christianity* (New York: Harper & Row, 1953); Roland H. Bainton, *Here I Stand: A Life of Martin Luther* (New York: Mentor Books, 1950); George Brantl, ed., *Catholicism* (New York: George Braziller, 1962); Henry Chadwick, *The Early Church* (New York: Viking Penguin, Inc., 1969); R. W. Southern, *The Making of the Middle Ages* (New Haven: Yale University Press, 1953); C. Warren Hollister, *Medieval Europe: A Short History,* 6th ed. (New York: McGraw-Hill Pub. Co., 1990); John Cogley, *Catholic America* (Garden City, NY: Doubleday & Co., Inc., 1960); Robert G. Clouse, Richard V. Pierard, and Edwin M. Yamauchi, *Two Kingdoms: The Church and Culture through the Ages* (Chicago: Moody Press, 1993).

Christ, also Jesus, Jesus Christ, the Messiah, Savior, Lord:
the son of God who came to earth for the purpose of becoming the
Savior of all mankind; He was faced with temptations ("common to
man") but lived a sinless life, living thirty-three years in the area of
modern Israel; the Nicene Creed* aptly summarizes the essence of
who Christ was and what His earthly mission was about:

We believe in one God, the Father Almighty, maker of heaven
and earth, of all that is seen and unseen. We believe in one Lord
Jesus Christ, the only begotten Son of God, begotten of His
Father before all worlds, God of God, Light of Light, very God
of very God, begotten, not made, being of one substance with
the Father, by whom all things were made; who for us men and
for our salvation, came down from heaven, and was incarnate
by the Holy Spirit of the Virgin Mary, and was made man. For
our sake he was crucified under Pontius Pilate. He suffered and
was buried. On the third day he rose again in accordance with
the Scriptures; he ascended into heaven and is seated at the
right hand of the Father. He will come again, with glory, to
judge the living and the dead; whose kingdom shall have no
end. We believe in the Holy Spirit, the Lord, and the Giver of
Life, who proceeds from the Father and the Son. With the
Father and the Son he is worshipped and glorified. He has
spoken through the Prophets. We believe in one holy catholic
and apostolic Church. We acknowledge one baptism for the
forgiveness of sins. We look for the resurrection of the dead,
and the life of the world to come. Amen.

Although He was the only perfect person ever to live, He was falsely
accused and subsequently tried and crucified by angry and jealous men;
because of His love for the human race Christ chose to come to earth,
fully aware of His cruel and impending death; His death by crucifixion
was His gift to all people, that they might have eternal life and join Him
in heaven after death, that is, if only they would put their trust and faith
in Him; His crucifixion was symbolic not only for the first century AD,
but for all eras, covering all sin, even yours; according to His teachings,
every person has sinned or will sin and must ask Him for forgiveness in

order to enter heaven after death; Christ is the only historic person to rise from the dead, a fact witnessed by a large group of people in Jerusalem and recorded by four of His close associates (Matthew 28; Mark 16; Luke 24; and John 20); through His sinless life, His pain-filled death, and His Resurrection, Christ conquered sin and death so that whoever chooses to place faith in Him may gain eternal life*, and experience "abundant life" while on earth; Christ said, "I came that they might have life, and have it to the full" (John 10:10); the first four books of the New Testament*, the Gospels ("good news"), are contemporary accounts of Christ's life and teachings. The late P. Carnegie Simpson cogently states:

> We had thought intellectually to examine him; we find he is spiritually examining us. The roles are reversed between us. . . . We study Aristotle and are intellectually edified thereby; we study Jesus and are, in the profoundest way, spiritually disturbed . . . We are constrained to take up some inward moral attitude of heart and will in relation to this Jesus . . . A man may study Jesus with intellectual impartiality, he cannot do it with moral neutrality . . . We must declare our colours. To this has our unevasive contact with Jesus brought us. We began it in the calm of the study; we are called out of the field of moral decision (*The Fact of Christ*, 1930; James Clarke edition, 1956, 23–34).

Bibl: "Christ's Person" and "Christ's Work" in John R. W. Stott, *Basic Christianity* (London: InterVarsity Press, 1958), 21–60, 81–105 passim; C. S. Lewis, *Mere Christianity* (New York: The Macmillan Co., 1952); and *Miracles: A Preliminary Study* (New York: The Macmillan Co., 1947); Frank Morison, *Who Moved the Stone?* (London: Faber and Faber, 1958); J. Dwight Pentecost, A *Harmony of the Words and Works of Jesus Christ* (Grand Rapids, MI: Zondervan Pub. House, 1981); Thomas á Kempis (d. 1471), *Imitation of Christ*, trans. by Ronald Knox (1960; repr., South Bend, IN: Greenlawn Press, 1990); Simon Greenleaf, *The Testimony of the Evangelists* (Grand Rapids, MI: Baker Book House, 1965); John A. Broadus, *Jesus of Nazareth* (Grand Rapids, MI: Baker Book House, 1963); Robert Glenn Gromacki, *The Virgin Birth* (New York:

Thomas Nelson, Inc., 1974); Wilbur Smith, *Have You Considered Him?* (Downers Grove, IL: InterVarsity Press, 1970).

Christendom: a term referring to the consolidation of all culture—politics, art, music, education—around the unifying center of Christian faith; such a unification has been more an ideal than a reality in church history, although the era from 1000–1300 in European history manifested the closest approximation to this ideal; in American history, elements of Christendom can be found in Puritan New England (1620–1700) and following the Second Great Awakening (revival) (1825–50); some elements of the contemporary Christian Right Movement aspire to see the establishment of an evangelical "Christendom" in America today.

Bibl: Martin Marty, *Christendom* (New York: Harper-Row, 1982); Martin Marty, *Righteous Empire: The Protestant Experience in America* (New York: Harper & Row, 1970).

Christianity: the religion derived from the life and teachings of Christ and based on the Bible*; a worldwide religion with three main divisions: Protestantism*, Roman Catholicism*, and Orthodoxism*.

Bibl: John R. W. Stott, *Basic Christianity* (London: InterVarsity Press, 1958); Josh McDowell, *The New Evidence That Demands a Verdict* (Nashville: Nelson Reference, 1999); D. James Kennedy, *Knowing the Whole Truth: Basic Christianity and What It Means in Your Life* (Old Tappan, NJ: Fleming H. Revell Co., 1976); W. H. C. Frend, *The Rise of Christianity* (Philadelphia: Fortress Press, 1984); Edwin Yamauchi, *Harper's World of the New Testament* (San Francisco: Harper & Row, 1981); Francis A. Schaeffer, *The Complete Works of Francis A. Schaeffer: A Christian Worldview*, 5 vols. (Westchester, IL: Crossway Books, 1968–1982); J. N. D. Anderson, *Christianity: The Witness of History* (London: Tyndale Press, 1969); see early church*.

convert: (from Latin *converte,* to turn around, transform) one who has made a definite and decisive choice to become a Christian;

i.e., to turn around one's life from a course leading to eternal punishment in hell* to one directed toward eternal life* and joy in heaven*, and at the same time, experience a transformation in one's spiritual outlook; see salvation*, saved*, sanctification*, Christian*.

Bibl: Josh McDowell, "He Changed My Life," in *The New Evidence That Demands a Verdict* (Nashville: Nelson Reference, 1999); Bill Bright, *Jesus and the Intellectual* (Campus Crusade for Christ International, 1968); Nicky Cruz, *Run Baby Run* (Plainfield, NJ: Logos Books, 1968); movie version, *The Cross and the Switchblade*, available at Christian bookstores*); C. S. Lewis, *Mere Christianity* (New York: The Macmillan Co., 1952); Roger Staubach, *Staubach: First Down, Lifetime to Go* (Waco, TX: Word Inc., 1974); Charles Colson, *Born Again* (Old Tappan, NJ: Revell, 1977); E. Stanley Jones, *Conversion* (New York: Abingdon Press, 1959); Richard Wurmbrand, *Tortured for Christ* (Glendale, CA: Diane Books, 1967).

creed: a succinct authoritative statement of religious belief; a brief formal summary of the Christian faith (Oxford English Dictionary); "a fixed formula summarizing the essential articles of the Christian religion and enjoying the sanction of ecclesiastical authority" J. N. D. Kelly, *Early Christian Creeds* (London, Longman, 1972).

Bibl: see canon* and Christianity*.

cult: a religion that is not orthodox*; several religions have taken on some of the tenets of Christianity*, thereby gaining adherents by promoting what "appears" to be Christian but which, in fact, is a disguised false religion; e.g., Mormonism, Jehovah's Witnesses, Christian Science.

Bibl: Walter Martin, *The Kingdom of the Cults* (Minneapolis: Bethany House, 1985). It is distinguished from a "sect," a splinter group that parts company with a larger church denomination* as an expression of its desire for purity of doctrine* or practice. A sect retains orthodox* beliefs; a cult rejects some aspect of historic Christianity* in its doctrine*.

Dead Sea Scrolls: a collection of ancient manuscripts which include the oldest known copies of the Old Testament* books in their original language, Hebrew; these documents date between the late third-century BC to AD 68 and were chronicled and later hidden near the extinct Essene community on the north shore of the Dead Sea, untouched until their discovery in 1947; less than one-fourth of the documents have been translated.

Bibl: Edwin Yamauchi, *The Stones and the Scriptures* (Grand Rapids, MI: Baker Book House, 1981), 126–145; F. F. Bruce, "The Dead Sea Scrolls and Early Christianity," *Bulletin of the John Rylands Library* 49 (1966); "Dead Sea Scrolls," ISBE, vol. 1, 883–897.

denomination: a number of local congregations which have united in a single legal and administrative body and thereby form a religious organization. The Protestant church (Protestantism) consists of numerous denominations informally referred to as the Baptists, Nazarenes, Free Methodists, United Methodists, Wesleyans, Presbyterians, Lutherans, etc.

Bibl: Frank S. Mead, *Handbook of Denominations,* 2nd ed. (New York: Abingdon Press, 1961); Sydney E. Ahlstrom, *A Religious History of the American People*, 2 vols. (Garden City, NY: Doubleday & Co. Inc., 1975).

Devil: (from Greek *diabolos,* slanderer) the synonym in the NT for the Hebrew word "Satan," a fallen angel named "Lucifer" who was cast out of heaven and who is the instigator of all evil on earth; Luke 10:18, Mark 3:27; see Satan*.

disciple: a Christian who believes in, commits to, and assists in the spreading of Christian doctrines* (Matthew 28:19; Acts 6:1).

Disciples: the twelve followers of Christ* belonging to His inner circle; they received instruction and practice in ministry and had intimate association with Christ* for around three years; for a list of the disciples: Mark 3:14f, 16:20; Matthew 10:1; Luke 6:13; John 2:11; see apostle*.

discipleship: an indoctrination and learning process new Christians should go through en route to a more mature spiritual level; an accountability process usually monitored by a mature Christian.

Bibl: Dietrich Bonhoeffer, *The Cost of Discipleship* (New York: Macmillan Pub. Co., 1937); Thomas á Kempis, *The Imitation of Christ*, trans. by Ronald Knox (1960; repr., South Bend, IN: Greenlawn Press, 1990); Walter A. Henrichsen, *Disciples are Made, Not Born* (SP Pub., 1988); Jerry Bridges, *The Pursuit of Holiness* (Colorado Springs, CO: NavPress, 1978).

doctrine: an established position or body of principles held as the authoritative beliefs of a religious organization or denomination*.

Bibl: John Lawson, *Introduction to Christian Doctrine* (Grand Rapids, MI: Zondervan Pub. House, 1967); Shirley C. Guthrie, Jr., *Christian Doctrine: Teachings of the Christian Church* (Atlanta: John Knox Press, 1968).

early church: a term anachronistically used in reference to the collective NT* congregations.

Bibl: Henry Chadwick, *The Early Church* (New York: Viking Penguin, Inc., 1969); Philip Schaff, *History of the Christian Church* (Grand Rapids, MI: William B. Eerdmans Pub. Co., 1962); John Warwick Montgomery, *History of Christianity* (Downers Grove, IL: InterVarsity Press, 1972); see Christianity*.

entire sanctification: a belief held by some denominations* that a decisive stage exists in the ongoing process of being filled with and empowered by the Holy Spirit*; a recognized time in a mature Christian's life when he or she invites the Holy Spirit* to take power over all areas of the person's life (1 Thessalonians 3:12–13, 5:23–24).

eternal life: for Christians, an infinite time of abiding fellowship with God and other Christians after one's life here on earth ends; syn.—"everlasting life."

eternal security: a belief held by some Christians that persons who have truly trusted in Christ for salvation* can never lose that salvation* by any act or decision of their own will; also known as perseverance of the saints*; this view, held by Calvinists and many Baptist denominations, is based upon Scripture texts like John 10:28 and Romans 8:38, 39 and a logical argument that contends that persons born into the family of God can never be "unborn"; adherents to this view place a strong emphasis upon God's sovereign act in salvation*—an act that cannot be nullified by any human act; opponents of this view—known as Arminians or Wesleyans—contend that God's sovereign power does not remove human freedom; while no other human or superhuman power can separate us from God's love, we still have the capability of rejecting God's grace by a conscious act of the will; the truth likely lies some place between the Calvinist emphasis upon God's sovereign power and the Arminian emphasis upon human freedom and responsibility.

Bibl: Guy Duty, *If Ye Continue* (Minneapolis: Bethany House, 1998); Robert Shank, *Life in the Son* (Minneapolis: Bethany House, 1989); J. F. Strombeck, *Shall Never Perish* (Strombeck Agency, 1975); Clarence Bence, *Romans* (Indianapolis: Wesleyan Publishing House, 1996).

eucharist: (from Greek *eucharidzo,* to give thanks) a term for the Lord's Supper or Holy Communion most often used in liturgical churches like Episcopalian, Lutheran, or Roman Catholic*; originates from the Apostle Paul's* description of the original Last Supper in 1 Corinthians 12: "after supper, he took the bread and when he had given thanks, he gave it to them."

evangelical: (from Greek *euangelion,* good news, gospel) a person or position emphasizing the authority of Scripture (esp. the Gospels), salvation* by faith* in Christ* through personal conversion, and committed to leading non-Christians to salvation* through personal encounter.

Bibl: Leighton Ford, *The Christian Persuader: The Urgency of Evangelism in Today's World* (Minneapolis, MN: World Wide

Publications, 1966); Robert E. Coleman, *The Master Plan of Evangelism* (Old Tappan, NJ: Fleming H. Revell Co., 1963); Bill Bright, *Have You Heard of the Four Spiritual Laws?* (Campus Crusade For Christ, 1965).

Evangelical: a person holding evangelical* principles; a member of an evangelical church; often associated with fundamentalism.

Bibl: Keith J. Hardman, *The Spiritual Awakeners* (Chicago: Moody Press, 1983).

faith: (from Latin *fides,* trust, akin to Latin *fidere,* to trust) *noun* having loyalty to and belief and trust in God and His truths—recorded in the Bible*; syn. loyalty; *verb* a believing with strong conviction in a system of religious doctrines*; syn. belief; Hebrews 11:1–3; see saved* and salvation*.

Bibl: John White, "Prayer" in *The Fight* (Downers Grove, IL: InterVarsity Press, 1976), 19–37; John White, *Daring to Draw Near* (Downers Grove, IL: InterVarsity Press, 1977).

Fall: Adam and Eve's act of disobedience in the Garden of Eden and the resulting consequences of that act. Although Eve and Adam had the freedom not to sin*, they chose, by a free act of their will, to disobey God's commands. As a result, they lost the intimate relationship they had enjoyed with God and became accountable for all their moral actions. The consequences of their act affected human relationships, family structure, even the natural order. After the Fall, sin* and suffering were a "given" of the created order (Genesis 3:14–19). Furthermore, human beings are inclined from birth to be self-centered and resistant to God.

fornication: (from Latin *fornix,* brothel) a sin occurring when two people other than husband and wife have sexual intercourse; a term usually applied to a sexual encounter between two unmarried participants (if at least one of the participants is married, adultery* is also taking place); see adultery*.

fruit of the Spirit: a metaphorical phrase denoting the virtues manifest in the ideal Christian life, resulting from the indwelling (in a person's being) of the Holy Spirit*; the "fruit of the Spirit" is generally accepted as those virtues so designated in Galatians 5:22–26.

Bibl: Gene A. Getz, The *Measure of a Man* (Glendale, CA: Regal Pub., 1974); and *The Measure of a Woman* (Ventura, CA: Regal Pub., 1984).

gospel: (from the Old English *good-spell* meaning "good news") The Greek word *euangelion* is similarly translated. The good news refers to the teaching of Jesus concerning forgiveness and the account of His saving work on the cross. The early writers— Matthew, Mark, Luke, and John—of the New Testament adopted this term to describe their narratives of Jesus' life and death. The term evangelical* derives from this same term.

grace: (from Latin *gratia*, favor) (1) an unmerited favor from God; unmerited divine help which God affords man for regeneration and sanctification*; a working definition comes when contrasted with mercy*—"grace is getting what one does not deserve while mercy is not getting what one does deserve"; (2) a God-given virtue.

Great Judgment Day: God's final judgment of mankind at the end of the world (2 Corinthians 5:10, Revelation 20:11–15, John 12:48).

Hades: In Greek mythology, the "underworld" or place of the dead. Given its pagan origins, this place was associated with dread and gloom. The New Testament* writers sometimes used this term to describe the kingdom of death, ruled by Satan* and his forces. In the Apostles' Creed*, the reference to Christ* descending into hell* refers to this realm of darkness, not to the eternal lake of fire (Gehenna) reserved for all the wicked at the end of history.

heathen: a non-Christian member of a people who do not acknowledge God; a term often used in the context of the uncivilized or irreligious.

heaven: (from Hebrew *samayim,* heights, and *marom,* height, Greek *ouranos,* that which is raised up) a spiritual realm where Christians abide with God after their life on earth has ended; a place absent of sin* and sorrow enjoyed only by holy beings, including hosts of angels, Christians, and God; the OT* usually infers, metaphorically at least, that heaven is a fixed and material place (Genesis 7:11; Job 26:11; 2 Samuel 22:8); and Christ* does the same in John 14; the NT* writers often infer that heaven is synonymous with authority (Matthew 3:16–17; Acts 26:19); the prophetic Scriptures (eschatological) indicate that heaven (or the heavens) will be remade at the end of this present age; i.e., when evil is destroyed (Isaiah 51:6, 65:17, 66:22; Matthew 24:29; Ephesians 6:12).

hell: (from Greek *Gehenna,* derived from Hebrew *hinnom,* a valley flanking Jerusalem where children were burned as sacrifices during pagan rites) the devil's* wicked realm where non-Christians go for eternal punishment after their life on earth has ended; the devil* himself will be punished here (the lake of fire) at the end of the world.

Bibl: D. James Kennedy, "He Descended into Hell" in *Knowing the Whole Truth: Basic Christianity and What It Means in Your Life* (Old Tappan, NJ: Fleming H. Revell Co., 1976), 69–76.

heresy: (from Greek *haireo,* to take, to select) a religious doctrine* or dogma contrary to orthodoxy* and sound biblical teaching; the term often refers to a recognized movement based on heretical teachings; most modern-day cults* are considered to be heretical movements; a "heretic" (hairetikos) is an adherent of a heresy.

Bibl: F. F. Bruce, *The Defense of the Gospel in the New Testament* (Grand Rapids, MI: William B. Eerdmans Publishing Co., 1959); see cult*.

holiness: (from Hebrew *qados,* derived from *qd,* to cut or separate, apartness; Greek *hagios*) the separation of something or someone from the profane or common to God's use; a term used in reference to things or persons separated for God and His service; God's character is the antithesis of the world's, and He would not be God without being holy; Hebrews 2:11, 12:10; John 17:19; in the NT*, Christians are often referred to as "saints" (hagioi).

Bibl: Jerry Bridges, *The Pursuit of Holiness* (Colorado Springs, CO: NavPress, 1978); John White, "Holiness" in *The Fight* (Downers Grove, IL: InterVarsity Press, 1976), 177–199.

Holy Spirit or Spirit: (from Greek *pneuma,* wind, breath, life) part of the Godhead, i.e., the Father (God), Son (Christ)*, and Holy Ghost (Spirit) which empowers Christians for God's service; Geoffrey W. Bromiley, a renowned biblical scholar, asserts that in Matthew and Mark, "The Spirit is God's power making possible speech and action that are beyond human resources. The phenomena of the Spirit are subordinate to the realization that the messianic age has dawned. They have a christological reference"; and in reference to St. Paul's* NT* writings, Bromiley asserts:

The Spirit manifests Christ's saving work and makes responsible acceptance of it possible. Hence *pneuma* denotes both God's Spirit and the innermost being of those who no longer live by the self but by God's being for them" (*Theological Dictionary of the New Testament,* abridged edition, [Grand Rapids, MI: William B. Eerdmans, 1985], 886–887, 891).

icthus: (transliteration of Greek *icthus,* fish) a symbol and acronym used by the early Christian community to signify belief in Christ*, and in turn, adopted by the present generation; e.g., fish symbols were found on Christian tombs and hiding places in antiquity, and today people put fish symbols on cars, notebooks, etc.; icthus is acronymic for Jesus, Christ*, God's Son (both words), Savior; thus ICTHUS, the Greek equivalent of these letters, is often found within the fish symbol; Christ's metaphorical use of "fishers of men" and His miracles involving fish serve as the basis for the icthus symbol (Matthew 7:10; 14:17; Mark 6:38; Luke 5:6, 9:13; John 6:9, 21:5–11).

idolatry: (from Greek *eidolon,* idol, phantom, akin to Greek *eidos,* form) the worship of any physical object as a god; a sin* targeted in the Ten Commandments; Christianity* is monotheistic*, and any adherence to a god created by man not only violates the worship of God, the one and true God and Creator of all things, but defies rational thought.

incarnation: (from Latin *carnus,* flesh) the Christian belief that the Son, the second person of the Trinity*, assumed human flesh and blood and entered history as a human being, born of the Virgin Mary about 2,000 years ago (John 1:14); orthodox* teaching holds that Jesus retained His divine nature (surrendering some of His glory and divine attributes) while at the same time becoming truly human in every way (Philippians 2:6–8), except that He existed without a fallen nature and never succumbed to the temptation to sin (Hebrews 4:15); as the "God-man," He is the perfect Redeemer of the human race.

Bibl: Lee Strobel, *The Case for Christ* (Grand Rapids, MI: Zondervan, 1998).

indulgence: a Roman Catholic practice of granting official pardon (remission) of sins*, based on the belief that after one sins and the guilt has been forgiven, a debt is owed to God; the Roman Catholic Church* claims authority to grant such a remission because of its Apostolic succession; George Brantl, a Catholic scholar, writes, "The power of the [Catholic] Church to grant indulgences follows from the powers the Church claims as the Body of Christ on earth"; Catholicism draws on the spiritual treasury endowed by surplus merits of Christ, His mother Mary, and the saints—a principle known in Catholic teachings as "vicarious satisfaction," which also asserts that a sinner is never able to do sufficient penance to extinguish the guilt incurred by sin* (expiation) and, therefore, must appeal to the pope, cardinal or bishop; only the pope can grant indulgences for the dead; indulgences are only granted to members of the Catholic

Church*; a "plenary" (from Latin *plenus,* full) indulgence remits the entire payment of punishment due, whereas a "partial" indulgence only satisfies part of the debt; this suspect doctrine* rests on various other "added" canonical doctrines* (papal decrees); e.g., the doctrine* of "merits" contends that God promises to reward certain human acts done in His name and for His glory. During the Middle Ages the open abuse of granting indulgences for financial contributions to the church drew sharp criticism, most notably from Martin Luther, as postulated in his "Ninety-five Theses"; he revealed the nonscriptural basis of indulgences and touched off the Protestant Reformation*; in 1516 Luther declared:

No one can know whether the remission of sins is complete, because complete remission is granted only to those who exhibit worthy contrition and confession, and no one can know whether contrition and confession are perfectly worthy. To assert that the pope can deliver souls from purgatory is audacious. If he can do so, then he is cruel not to release them all. But if he possesses this ability, he is in a position to do more for the dead than for the living. The purchasing of indulgences in any case is highly dangerous and likely to induce complacency. Indulgences can remit only those private satisfactions imposed by the Church, and may easily militate against interior penance, which consists in true contrition, true confession, and true satisfaction in spirit" (in Roland H. Bainton, *Here I Stand: A Life of Martin Luther* [New York: Mentor Books, 1950], 54).

After Luther's bold protest against the abuses of the Church in granting indulgences (release from purgatory* and hell* could be secured for payment of money in his day), the Roman Catholic Church* moderated its practices; however, the belief in and the practice of granting indulgences continues to this day in the Roman Catholic Church*.

Bibl: Bainton, *Here I Stand*; George Brantl, ed., *Catholicism* (New York: George Braziller, 1962), 232–237.

Judaism: the Jewish religion derived from that of the ancient Hebrews, who developed the first true monotheism (belief in one God only); Judaism's foundation is on God (Yahweh) who revealed himself to the Patriarchs (Abraham, Isaac, and Jacob, ca. 2000–1700 BC), Moses (ca. 1440 or 1270 BC) and the Hebrew prophets; conformity to the writings of Moses and the Prophets (OT*) and Jewish rites, ceremonies and traditions; Judaism was fully developed by AD 500, is legalistic, denies the divine attributes of Christ* and thus discredits the NT, and is indelibly linked with its authoritative works: the Talmud (composed of the Mishnah and Gemara) and the Midrashim (official commentary on the OT* books); the fulcrum of Judaism is the Torah (rendered "law"; "instruction"; or "revelation"), with a main emphasis on the Pentateuch; although Judaism is rich in both culture and heritage, its rejection of Christ* as the Messiah and of the authenticity of the NT* books is ill-founded; Jewish jealousy of Christ* and animosity with early Christianity is documented in the NT* and extra-biblical references: Matthew 26:59–67, 27:11–26, 41–56; 27:57–28:20; Acts 6:8–7:60; Josephus, a Jewish historian for the Romans (a traitor), wrote ca. AD 93:

> Now, there was about this time, Jesus, a wise man, if it be lawful to call him a man, for he was a doer of wonderful works—a teacher of such men as receive the truth with pleasure. He drew over to him both many of the Jews, and many of the Gentiles. He was [the] Christ; and when Pilate, at the suggestion of the principal men amongst us [the Jews], had condemned him to the cross, those that loved him at the first did not forsake him, for he appeared to them alive again the third day, as the divine prophets had foretold these and ten thousand other wonderful things concerning him; and the tribe of Christians, so named from him, are not extinct at this Day" (*Antiquities of the Jews* 8.3.3).

The three main divisions of modern Judaism are: Orthodox Judaism, strictly observing the Torah and Talmud pursuant to an authoritative rabbinic law code; Conservative Judaism, also observing the Torah and Talmud, but allowing for adaptations for modern circumstances—the largest Jewish movement (prevalent movement in the USA); and Reform Judaism, advocating the removal of Talmudic restrictions. The Judaism of Christ's* era (early first century) was comprised of five major divisions: the Pharisees, Sadducees, Zealots, Essenes, and Samaritans.

Bibl: Arthur Hertzberg, ed., *Judaism* (New York: George Braziller, 1962).

justification: (from Latin *justus,* from *jus,* right, law) God's gracious and judicial act in which He bestows upon a sinner a full pardon of guilt and penalty of sins* committed, and accepts the recipients as righteous; when a person exclaims, "I'm saved!" he or she could properly pronounce, "I've been justified!"; in the conservative *Introduction to Theology,* an excellent definition of "justification" is given in comparison with "sanctification":

> Justification in a broad sense has reference to the whole work of Christ wrought for us; sanctification, the whole work wrought in us by the Holy Spirit.
> Justification is a judicial act in the mind of God; sanctification, a spiritual change wrought in the hearts of men.
> Justification is a relative change, that is, a change in relation from condemnation to favor; sanctification, an inward change from sin to holiness.
> Justification secures for us the remission of actual sins; sanctification, in its complete sense, cleanses the heart from original sin or inherited depravity.
> Justification removes the guilt of sin; sanctification destroys its power.
> Justification makes possible adoption into the family of God; sanctification restores the image of God.
> Justification gives a title to heaven; sanctification, a fitness for heaven.
> Justification logically precedes sanctification, which in its initial stage, is concomitant with it.
> Justification is an instantaneous and completed act and, therefore, does not take place in stages, or by degrees;

sanctification is marked by progressiveness in that partial or initial sanctification occurs at the time of justification, and entire sanctification occurs subsequent to justification. Both initial and entire sanctification, however, are instantaneous acts wrought in the hearts of men by the Holy Spirit. [This last point is hotly debated, and represents but one view of the process of sanctification.] H. Orton Wiley and Paul T. Culbertson, *Introduction to Christian Theology* (Kansas City: Beacon Hill Press, 1945), 313; see sanctification*.

King James Version (KJV): the prominent English translation of the Bible* until recent history, and easily recognized by its Old English prose; King James I of England authorized this translation to settle the dispute over existing translations; he decreed that a translation be made of the whole Bible*, as constant as could be to the original Hebrew and Greek, and this was to be set out and printed without any marginal notes and was only to be used in all Churches of England in time of Divine Service.

The KJV, first published in 1611, underwent many editions, numbering thousands of corrections; popular editions (revisions) of the KJV include "The Authorized Version" in 1769, though ipso facto unofficial, "The Revised Version" in 1885, "The American Standard Version" (of the Revised Version) in 1901, and the Revised Standard Version (RSV) in 1952, with an Expanded Edition in 1977; many churches prefer the KJV over other translations, mainly because of tradition, and perhaps because of the Old English prose, but many new Christians and the younger generation have difficulty with such wording; the RSV, considered the most accurate among the KJV revisions, proved unacceptable to a vast majority of American conservatives, a reaction which eventually culminated in the publication of The New International Version* in 1978 (the translation used in this book).

mercy: (from Latin *merces,* wages, price paid) a love which includes both pity and compassion and which God exercises toward undeserving people (Matthew 9:36); see grace*.

millennium: (from Latin *mille* + *annum,* thousand years) a thousand-year reign of Christ on earth at the close of human history; described in detail in Revelation 20:1–6 and in more general terms by the Old Testament prophets; Christians who hold to a literal interpretation of these thousand years are divided between those who hold that the second coming* of Christ* occurs after this kingdom is established (post-millennialism) and those who believe that Christ* must return to earth before this righteous rule begins (pre-millennialism); a third group holds that biblical accounts of this reign of Christ* are to be understood figuratively as applying to His spiritual lordship in the life of believers and the church (a-millennialism).

Bibl: Robert Clouse, et. al., *The Meaning of the Millennium* (Downers Grove, IL: InterVarsity Press, 1978).

monotheism: (from Greek *monos*, alone, single + Greek *theos,* god) the belief that only one true god exists; Christianity* is monotheistic and has roots in Judaism* and the Jewish heritage; i.e., the monotheism of the ancient Hebrews—the first true monotheism.

naturalism: a philosophical perspective (worldview*) that presupposes the physical world is all that exists and that it is a closed system where all events derive from natural causes; naturalism rejects the existence of any supernatural being(s) and therefore espouses an atheistic* view of reality.

New International Version (NIV): a translation of the Bible* from the earliest extant Hebrew and Greek manuscripts, completed in 1978 by an international team of conservative Protestant scholars with a "high view of Scripture"; see King James Version*.

New Testament (NT): see Bible*.

Nicene Creed: a term most often used in reference to a creed* used by the modern Christian movement which, in essence, is derived from an official statement used in defense of orthodox* Christianity*, promulgated at the Council of Nicæa in AD 325—Emperor Constantine called the Church-wide meeting (council) to deal with heresies, specif. Arianism, that were threatening the unity of the Christian Church; ancient Nicæa (modern Isnik, Turkey) was conveniently close to Constantine's capital (Constantinople); see Christ*.

Old Testament (OT): see Bible*.

orthodox: (from Greek *orth,* straight, true; + *doxa,* opinion) (1) religious teachings and practices that conform to the established doctrine* of the Church, i.e., that do not contradict the essence of the Apostles' Creed*, the biblical canon*, and the officially approved doctrines* unique to the relative main movement of Christianity*; (2) a participant in, or relating to, the Orthodox Church*; a participant in, or relating to, Orthodox Judaism—see Judaism*.

Orthodox Church, specifically the Eastern Orthodox Church (OC): one of the three main divisions of Christianity*, it approaches religion through liturgy (rites prescribed to public worship), highly emphasizes the Trinity*, the infallibility of the Church, a strict adherence to traditions, the episcopate and priesthood, icons, and claims to have unbroken Apostolic succession—a claim rivaled by the Roman Catholic Church*; the organizational impetus occurred after Emperor Constantine moved the Roman Empire's capital to Constantinople (modern Istanbul, Turkey), and thus the center of Christendom* shifted from the Latin-speaking region to that of the Greeks, with four ancient patriarchates (the headquarters of a patriarch—OC leader) established at Constantinople, Alexandria, Antioch, and Jerusalem; today eight patriarchs are officially recognized—the four ancient patriarchs plus Russia, Romania, Serbia, and Bulgaria, and the Gregorian Church head dubbed "catholicos-patriarch," with "archbishop" and "metropolitan" reserved for all other heads of churches; the OC officially broke from the Roman Catholic Church* in 1054 (i.e., the Great Schism); the OC rejects the Roman Catholic doctrine* of papal infallibility; the OC takes great pride in its heritage, e.g., the seven great Church councils held between 325 and 787.

Bibl: R. W. Southern, *The Making of the Middle Ages* (New Haven: Yale University Press, 1953); George Ostrogorsky, *History of the Byzantine State* (New Brunswick, NJ: Rutgers University Press, 1969); Kenneth Scott Latourette, *A History of Christianity* (New York: Harper & Row, 1953); Henry Chadwick, *The Early Church* (New York: Viking Penguin, Inc., 1969); C. Warren Hollister, *Medieval Europe: A Short History*, 6th ed. (New York: McGraw-Hill Pub. Co., 1990).

pagan: (from Latin *paganus,* country dweller) (1) an irreligious person; one having little or no religion and who delights in worldly pleasures; (2) one believing in a polytheistic* religion, the norm for Roman society—the political and cultural context in which Christianity* was born.

Bibl: Ramsay MacMullen, *Christianizing the Roman Empire*: A.D. 100–400 (London: Yale University Press, 1984); Robin Lane Fox, *Pagans and Christians* (New York: Alfred A. Knopf, Inc., 1987).

paraphrase: a version of the Bible*, usually written by one person, designed to offer a loose translation of the original text in a form easily understood by the layperson; although easy to read and understand, these versions often sacrifice accuracy and scholarship for the sake of popular appeal; often written by one person who interjects personal bias and doctrinal views into the translation, these paraphrases lack the integrity of translations like the King James* and the New International (NIV)* versions of the Bible*. The most popular paraphrases are The Living Bible and The Message.

Paul (Apostle*): an Apostle* of Christ* who wrote over half of the NT* books; although not among the original twelve Apostles*, he radically converted from Judaism* to Christianity* while en route from Jerusalem to Damascus for the purpose of persecuting Christians (Acts 9:1–31); after his conversion, Paul (formerly Saul) became the most prominent spokesperson for the early church, enduring numerous hardships and persecutions while planting and encouraging new churches throughout Israel, Asia Minor and even into Europe; Paul was a Christian Jew and a Roman citizen; his successful endeavors for Christianity* and his exit from the Jewish religious sect of the Pharisees invoked the wrath of the Jewish leaders and eventually a series of events that would end his life (Acts 21–28); although the biblical account does not record Paul's death, a strong tradition records that he was beheaded by Nero.

Bibl: see Apostle*.

penance: (from Latin *poenitentia,* akin to *paenitentia,* regret) an action performed to show repentance or sorrow for sin; when St. Jerome translated the Bible* into Latin for the Roman Catholic Church* (the Vulgate), he chose "penance" as a rendering for NT words which actually denote "repentance"*, an error of leviathan importance; i.e., "penance" is an outward act, "repentance" an inward act of faith. Thus the foundational doctrine* of salvation* was radically altered, a mistake which would lend support to another tenuous doctrine*, indulgences*, and ultimately invoke the Protestant Reformation*. In the Roman Catholic* and Eastern Orthodox* churches (and some Anglican), a confessor (a local priest) listens to a sinner's confession, administers absolution (the remission of the guilt or consequences of the sin* confessed), and then chooses and assigns the appropriate penance.

Bibl: see indulgence* and Catholic Church*.

perseverance of the Saints: see eternal security*.

polytheism: (from Greek *poly,* many + *theos,* god) the worship of and belief in more than one god; the first of the Ten Commandments labels this a sin*—"You shall have no other gods before me [God]" (Exodus 20:7); see monotheism*.

Protestantism: one of the three main movements of Christianity* (along with the Orthodox* and Roman Catholic Churches*); a "protest" against the Roman Catholic Church* in the early sixteenth century produced a movement labeled as the "Protestants"; the sixteenth-century Protestants, led by Martin Luther, disagreed with many doctrines* and organizational corruption in the established

Church and initially attempted to change it from within; perhaps the paramount issue was doctrinaire, addressing the scriptural basis of salvation*—the Protestants championed "justification* by faith alone" (a scripturally sound doctrine*), whereas the Catholics stressed the necessity of penance*, the doctrine* of indulgences*, and the doctrine* of merits (all scripturally suspect).

Bibl: Bernard Ramm, *Protestant Christian Evidences* (Chicago: Moody Press, 1954); also see orthodox*, Catholic Church*, indulgence*, penance*, salvation*.

purgatory: (from Latin *purgatus,* purging) according to Roman Catholic* doctrine*, this is a place or state of temporary misery and suffering for Christians who died in God's grace, yet still owing debt for past sins*; Protestants reject this doctrine* because of its lack of scriptural support and its reliance on two other tenuous Roman Catholic* doctrines*—indulgences* and merits; George Brantl, a Catholic scholar, writes:

> Purgatory is a place or state in which are detained the souls of those who die in grace, in friendship with God, but with the blemish of venial sin or with temporal debt for sin unpaid. Here the soul is purged, cleansed, readied for eternal union with God in Heaven. The suffering of the soul in Purgatory is intense, yet it is a suffering in love: the souls in Purgatory are not turned from God; they are deprived of the vision of God but they are united with Him by love. Theirs is a twofold suffering, that of privation of God for a time and that of physical pain (*Catholicism* [New York: George Braziller, 1962], 23).

A Roman Catholic council officially decreed:

> And so if persons duly penitent die in the charity of God (i.e., in sanctifying grace) before they have satisfied by due works of penance for their sins and omissions, their souls are purified after death by the fires of purgatory . . . and the souls of those who have incurred no stain of sin after their

Baptism, and those souls, too, who though stained have been duly purged whether with their bodies or after separation from their bodies as we mentioned above, are straightway received into heaven and clearly behold God Himself in three divine Persons . . . And then the souls of those who die in actual mortal sin . . . straightway go down into hell (*Council of Florence*, 1415–45).

The doctrine* of purgatory is certainly suspect, besides its sheer lack of scriptural support; consider Luke 23:43; 2 Corinthians 5:6; Romans 8:38; Revelation 14:13; also see chapter 2 of this book, titled "Understanding the Basics: Salvation."

Bibl: Dante's vivid *Divine Comedy* is an imaginative account of hell and purgatory from the Catholic perspective.

Quadrilateral (Wesleyan): a teaching device attributed to John Wesley describing the four primary sources of religious authority— Scripture, reason, tradition, and experience; although Wesley always assigned priority to the Bible* in formulating Christian doctrine*, he acknowledged that beliefs are shaped by use of logic and empirical investigation, religious and cultural traditions, as well as one's own personal experience.

Bibl: Donald Thorsen, *The Wesleyan Quadrilateral* (Grand Rapids, MI: Zondervan, 1990).

rapture: a belief held by many evangelical* Christians that at an unknown time (Matthew 24:26–27, 36, 44) Christ* will appear in the clouds, and take both the living Christians and the resurrected bodies of dead Christians from the earth; the rapture is closely associated with the second coming* of Christ*, the latter occurring shortly after the rapture (1 Thessalonians 4:14–17; Hebrews 9:28; Revelation 1:7; Acts 1:9–11; Matthew 23:38–39, 26:64, Titus 2:13; James 5:7–8, John 14:1–3; 2 Peter 3:10–11); numerous theories exist about the chronology of events between the rapture and the Final Judgment of the world.

Bibl: H. Orton Wiley and Paul T. Culbertson, "The Second Coming of Christ" in *Introduction to Christian Theology* (Kansas City: Beacon Hill Press, 1945). For a reasoned view from a non-Arminian perspective, see Robert D. Van Kampen, *The Rapture Question Answered, Plain and Simple* (Grand Rapids, MI: Fleming H. Revell, 1997).

Reformation, specifically Protestant Reformation: the Western Christendom* movement (ca. 1500–1650) which began in earnest in 1517 when Martin Luther challenged papal authority, primarily because of the perverse doctrine* of indulgences*. Luther and the reformers correctly asserted that the Catholic Church* had drifted away from the Apostolic foundations; i.e., the scriptural basis for salvation*. Luther based his arguments on the Scriptures and proclaimed salvation* by grace* through faith* in Christ*, whereas the Catholic Church* held that salvation* came through works of righteousness (an erroneous doctrine* which served as the basis for the doctrine* of indulgences*); see Protestant* and indulgence*.

Bibl: Roland H. Bainton, *Here I Stand: A Life of Martin Luther* (New York: Mentor Books, 1950).

religion: (from Latin *religio,* reverence) (1) the worship and service of God; (2) conformity to an official or institutionalized system of beliefs.

Bibl: Sydney E. Ahlstrom, *A Religious History of the American People,* 2 vols. (Garden City, NY: Doubleday & Co. Inc., 1975).

repentance: (from L *repoenitere,* to have grief, to be sorry; but *repoenitere* is an errant rendering of the New Testament* Greek *metanoeo,* to change completely one's way of life) to be sorry for one's sin, accompanied by a change of action—an amendment of one's actions, a commitment to refrain from those sinful acts causing the apology and sorrow; Byron H. DeMent and Edgar W. Smith pose a succinct clarification of the repentance-penance problem:

The true NT idea of repentance is very difficult to express in other languages. The Latin version renders *metanoeo* by *poenitentiam agere* ("exercise penitence"). But "penitence" etymologically signifies "pain, grief, distress," rather than a change of thought and purpose. Thus there developed in Latin Christianity a tendency to present grief over sin rather than abandonment of sin as the primary idea of NT repentance. Since it was easy to make the transition from penitence to penance, Jesus and the apostles were represented as urging people to "do penance" (Lat. *poenitentiam agite*). Eng. "repent" is derived from Lat. *repoenitere* and inherits the problem of the Latin, making grief the principal idea and keeping in the background the fundamental NT conception of a change of mind (i.e., purpose) with reference to sin. But the exhortations of the ancient prophets, of Jesus, and of the apostles show that the change of mind is the dominant idea of the words employed, while the accompanying grief and reform of life are necessary consequences," (*ISBE*, "Repent", vol. 4: 136); see Christian*.

Roman Catholicism: see Catholic Church*.

sacraments: religious observances, usually done in the context of worship, where tangible symbols are used to point to spiritual truths of the Christian faith; as many as seven sacraments have been identified by some traditions—Roman Catholicism being the primary one—of Christianity*; they include baptism, confirmation, Eucharist*, marriage, ordination, penance*, and extreme unction (or last rites); Protestants* have generally accepted only two sacraments—baptism and the Lord's supper—pointing out that these were the only two ordinances commanded by Christ* Himself; some Protestant* denominations* add foot-washing as a third sacrament instituted by Christ*.

Bibl: Rob Staples, *Outward Sign and Inward Grace* (Kansas City: Beacon Hill Press, 1991).

saint: a holy person; used originally in the New Testament* to refer to any believer in Christ* (Romans 1:7; Ephesians 1:1); early

Christians attributed special honor (veneration) upon those who were martyrs for the faith, eventually restricting the term to only those persons who had been judged by the official church as worthy of such a title; the Orthodox* and Catholic* branches of Christianity* teach that these designated persons of great holiness are to be venerated, but not worshipped; because of their special divine favor, they serve as advocates to God on behalf of Christians; it is therefore appropriate to pray to saints asking them to intercede on behalf of human needs. Protestants* have rejected the Catholic* understanding of saints and refer to all true believers who are pursuing godliness as "saints."

Bibl: Howard Harper, *Days and Customs of all Faiths* (New York: Fleet Publishing, 1977).

salvation: deliverance from the power and consequences of sin*; a necessary experience to assure entrance into heaven* after death, made possible by Christ's* life, death, and Resurrection, and that occurs when one places faith in Christ* and His teachings (e.g., Romans 3:23, 10:9; John 1:12, 3:3, 16, 36, 10:10, 14:6; Acts 17:30); see justification* and saved*.

sanctification: (from Latin *sanctus,* holy + *facere,* to make, based on Hebrew *qds,* set apart, brightness and Greek *hagiasmos,* holiness) the state of growing in God's grace* and being empowered with the Holy Spirit* as a result of Christian commitment after conversion; the Holy Spirit* is the active force in man's sanctification, working through God's Word (the Bible*), man's faith* (Ephesians 5:26; Hebrews 12:14); "Faith, itself produced by the Spirit, lays hold of the sanctifying resources," contends G. Walters, who also asserts:

As justification implies deliverance from the penalty of sin, so sanctification implies deliverance from the pollutions, privations and potency of sin. As to the intensity and extensiveness and steps of this latter deliverance, however, there is much discussion. The prayer that God will sanctify the believers wholly so that their whole spirit, soul and body be preserved blameless unto the coming of Christ is followed by the assertion that 'He who calls you is faithful, and he will do it' (1 Thessalonians 5:23–24)" (in *The New Bible* Dictionary*, 1069).

John Wesley, the founder of Methodism, offers the following comments on sanctification:

Q. What is it to be sanctified?
A. To be renewed in the image of God, in righteousness and true holiness.
   (*The Works of John Wesley*, vol. 8. [Grand Rapids, MI: Baker Book House, 1978], 279).

By justification we are saved from the guilt of sin, and restored to the favour of God; by sanctification we are saved from the power and root of sin, and restored to the image of God. All experience, as well as Scripture, show this salvation to be both instantaneous and gradual. It begins the moment we are justified, in the holy, humble, gentle, patient love of God and man. It gradually increases from that moment . . ." (Ibid., vol. 6:50); see justification*.

Satan: (from Greek *satanas,* adversary) the prince of evil and adversary of Christ*, and everything that is good; always hostile to God and continually working to overthrow God's purposes; but the NT* clearly outlines the limits of Satan's power and his ultimate destination; God places limits on his power (1 Corinthians 10:13; Revelation 20:2–10; Matthew 25:41; John 6:11; Hebrews 2:14; 1 John 3:8); Christ* commissioned the Apostle* Paul* to open people's eyes "and turn them from darkness to light, and from the power of Satan to God, so that they might receive forgiveness of sins and a place among those who are sanctified by faith in me" (Acts 26:18); see Devil*.

saved: in common usage the term is used to signify the act of becoming a Christian; if someone has been converted, they have, through faith*, turned from sin* to salvation*; i.e., they have been saved. "For it is by grace you have been saved, through faith—and this not from yourselves, it is the gift of God—not by works, so that no one can boast" (Ephesians 2:8); see salvation* and justification*.

second coming: the Christian belief that Jesus Christ* will return to this earth in a visible and physical form at the end of history; this doctrine* is the "blessed hope" (Titus 2:13) of all believers; Jesus promised to return for His church (John 14:2) and the disciples* who saw Him ascend were told that He would return in the same way as He had departed (Acts 10:11); there is considerable discussion among Christians about the timing and circumstances surrounding this event, but it is one of the orthodox* beliefs of all Christians.

Bibl: G. Elton Ladd, *The Blessed Hope* (Grand Rapids, MI: Eerdmans, 1978); Hal Lindsey, *The Late Great Planet Earth* (New York: Harper, 1963). A popular novel series (1999–2003) is the *Left Behind* series by Jerry Jenkins and Tim LaHaye (Wheaton, IL: Tyndale).

sin: a violation of the law of God; several NT* words are used in reference to "sin," e.g., *hamartia,* which denotes a deviation from the course or end appointed by God; John R. W. Stott, a popular Christian author, offers a useful discussion of sin:

But what is sin? Its universal extent is clear; what is its nature? Several words are used in the Bible to describe it. They group themselves into two categories, according to whether wrongdoing is regarded negatively or positively. Negatively, it is a shortcoming. One word represents it as a lapse, a slip, a blunder. Another pictures it as the failure to hit a mark, as when badness, a disposition which falls short of what is good. Positively, sin is transgression. One word makes sin the trespass of a boundary. Another reveals it as lawlessness, and another as an act which violates justice. Both these groups of words imply the existence of a moral standard. It is either an ideal which we fail to reach, or a law we break. 'Whoever knows what is right to do and fails to do it, for him it is sin,' says James [1:19–27].

That is the negative aspect. 'Every one who commits sin is guilty of lawlessness; sin is lawlessness,' says John [1 John 3:4–6]. That is the positive aspect (*Basic Christianity* [London: InterVarsity Press, 1958], 63–64; see also "The Fact and Nature of Sin" and "The Consequences of Sin," 1–80 passim).

theology: (from Greek *the(os),* God + *logia,* from logos, word, study) the study of the doctrine* of God; the study of God and His interaction with His creation;

"Man, inasmuch as he is able with his finite mind, trying to understand that which is infinite—the mind of God," Dr. Glenn Martin (Professor of History and Political Science, Indiana Wesleyan University.)

Bibl: Millard J. Erickson, *Concise Dictionary of Christian Theology* (Grand Rapids, MI: Baker Book House, 1986); Helmut Thelieke, *A Little Exercise for Young Theologians* (Grand Rapids, MI: Wm. B. Eerdmans Pub. Co., 1962). For a look at practical applications and issues, see Keith Drury, *So, What Do You Think?: Provocative Essays for Christians Who Think* (Indianapolis: Wesleyan Publishing House, 1998). For theological implications on scholarship, see Mark Noll, *The Scandal of the Evangelical Mind* (Grand Rapids, MI: Wm B. Eerdmans, 1994).

Trinity: (from Latin *tri* + *unitas,* tri-unity) one Godhead comprised of three equal parts (persons) in unity—the Father, Son, and Holy Spirit*; the term is based on but not found in the Scriptures—it came in the second century AD from Tertullian; the doctrine* of the Trinity is, nonetheless,

. . . the distinctive and all-comprehensive doctrine of the Christian faith. It makes three affirmations: that there is but one God, that the Father, the Son and the Spirit is each God, and that the Father, the Son and the Spirit is each a distinct Person. In this form it has become the faith of the church since it received its first full formulation at the hands of

Tertullian, Athanasius and Augustine" (R. A. Finlayson, *New Bible Dictionary*, 1221).
A conservative book on Christian theology asserts:

The doctrine of the Trinity which holds that there are three Persons in the one Godhead is one of the most sacred truths of the Christian Church . . . God the Father sent His Son into the world to redeem us; and God the Holy Spirit applies the redemptive work to our souls. The Trinity is therefore vitally involved in the work of salvation, and it is from this practical and religious aspect of the doctrine that the truth must be sought. The early Christians saw that if Christ was not divine they could not worship Him without becoming idolaters. On the other hand, He had saved them, and through Him had come the gift of the Holy Spirit. They recognized, therefore, that He must be divine (H. Orton Wiley and Paul T. Culbertson, *Introduction to Christian Theology* [Kansas City: Beacon Hill Press, 1945], 110).

Also consult: Matthew 11:27, 28:19; John 10:30, 14:9–11, 20:28; Colossians 2:9; 1 John 5:20; Luke 3:22; Acts 2:33, 38, 8:16; Romans 8:26–27, 34; Galatians 4:6; 1 Corinthians 12:4–6; 2 Corinthians 13:14; Ephesians 4:4–6; 1 Peter 1:2; Jude 20–21.

worldview: the sum total of one's beliefs about the world that directs daily decisions and actions; a well-defined worldview has internal coherence and consistency whether that worldview is consciously or unconsciously maintained; the primary components of one's worldview address the questions of "what is real?" (ontology), "how does one know?" (epistemology), "what is right and good?" (axiology), and "where is history headed?" (teleology); a Christian worldview deals with the great doctrines* of creation, fall* and redemption, and eternal destiny.

Bibl: Charles Colson, *How Now Shall We Live?* (Wheaton, IL: Tyndale House, 1999); Ronald Nash, *Worldviews in Conflict* (Grand Rapids, MI: Zondervan, 1992); James Sire, *The Universe Next*

Door—A Basic Worldview Catalog (Downers Grove, IL: InterVarsity Press, 1997). For a more in-depth look at worldviews, see *The Complete Works of Francis A. Schaeffer: A Christian Worldview*, 5 vols. (Westchester, IL: Crossway Books, 1968–1982).

about the authors and artist

J. Bradley Garner has spent most of his professional career working in public schools as a teacher, school psychologist, and administrator. His primary work has been related to developing strategies for integrating people with disabilities into their local community through school, work, and relationships. He earned bachelor and master degrees from the University of Akron (1967, 1971) and a doctorate from Kent State University (1993). He also has done postdoctoral study through Trinity Evangelical Divinity Seminary. Brad is the co-author of two previous books that focus on employment and people with disabilities. His first book, *Getting Employed, Staying Employed*, was recognized and awarded by the President's Committee on the Employment of People with Disabilities. He also has authored several journal articles and book chapters, and speaks throughout North America on strategies for meeting the needs of students with learning and behavioral challenges. Dr. Garner teaches courses at Indiana Wesleyan University, in special education and the highly successful first-year course, "Becoming World Changers." If you have a conversation with Brad, it won't take him very long to tell you how much fun he is having and how wonderful his students are.

Ron Mazellan, the book's illustrator, has over twenty years of experience in the advertising, book publishing, and entertainment industries. He has illustrated for such renowned companies as Universal Studios, Warner Brothers Pictures, CBS Television, Mattel, Focus on the Family, American Express, The Cannon Group, Pepsi, Princess Cruises, Radio City Music Hall, Samsung, Sheraton International, TV Guide, Westin Hotels, and the Disney Company. His works appear in over 200 books and with many noted authors and publishers, including Houghton Mifflin, Regal Books, Dutton Children's Books, Scholastic Books, Tyndale House, Word, and Zondervan. Ron graduated from Wheaton College (1981), and has an M.A. from California State University-Fullerton (1991). Ron complements the outstanding art faculty team at Indiana Wesleyan University, where he has received three Teacher of Excellence Awards. He also has received two EPA Journalism Awards. His work was recently featured in the Society of Illustrators 41st Annual Publication. His opening illustration in chapter 1 of *Straight Talk* is a featured art piece at his campus. Representing the first-year college experience, this illustration will appear in other books representing the same. *The Harmonica*, a children's book on the Holocaust, is one of Ron's more recent fully illustrated works (Charlesbridge, 2003).

Jerry Pattengale, (Ph.D., Miami University of Ohio) received the National Student Advocate Award from Houghton Mifflin and the National Resource Center (2000). During his seven years at Azusa Pacific University the students twice named him "Professor of the Year" and once "Honors Professor of the Year." Jerry's NEH Award took him to Greece, and while leading a private foundation he collaborated with the British Museum on manuscript presentations and co-produced the *Odyssey in Egypt* program (which became a top-ten most-visited website globally). His books include *Visible Solutions for Invisible Students*; *The Brief Guide to Objective Inquiry; The Motivated Student* (in press, McGraw-Hill) and *Helping Sophomores Succeed* (in press, Jossey Bass). He has also contributed to *The Anchor Bible Dictionary* series; *Great Events in History II: Human Rights*; *The Light of Discovery*; *A History of the Modern Olympics*; *Great Events in American History*; *World Empire* and various student success publications. His *The Accidental Author* blog has proven popular at *The Chronicle Tribune* and PBS included his story in its special, *Leading the Way out of Poverty* (2006, WIPB).

Jerry travels and speaks widely, from private campuses such as Colgate, Taylor, and Wheaton to public universities like Houston, Michigan, and South Florida. In 2007 he was an invited participant at the White House to discuss faith-based initiatives. He currently serves as an administrator at his alma mater, Indiana Wesleyan University.

Lisa Velthouse is a writer, speaker, and recent college graduate who challenges emerging generations to pursue excellence in their relationships with Christ. Named *Brio* magazine's "Brio Girl" for the year 2000, Lisa is a contributing writer on several projects and is the author of *Saving My First Kiss: Why I'm Keeping Confetti in My Closet* (Regal, 2003), a book she published while still in college. It has been well received and is featured at a variety of stores, including mass distributors such as Wal-Mart. Lisa cites her daily journaling regimen, college mentor, and literature and writing courses as a few of the reasons she has developed an inviting writing style at such a young age. She is a 2003 alumna of The John Wesley Honors College. Find out more about Lisa at http://www.lisavelthouse.com (accessed August 7, 2007).

about the contributors

Charlie Alcock served for several years as the youth pastor at a large vibrant church in San Diego. He is a requested speaker for youth rallies, conferences, camps, and retreats. He joined the ranks of religion professors in 2003 and currently serves as an Assistant Professor of Religion at Indiana Wesleyan University.

Dr. Clarence L. Bence is the author of *Romans, A Bible Commentary in the Wesleyan Tradition* (Wesleyan Publishing House, 1996) and currently serves as Vice President and Dean of the College of Arts and Sciences at Indiana Wesleyan University.

Dr. Chris Bounds is a theology professor in the Division of Religion and Philosophy at Indiana Wesleyan University. He completed his Ph.D. in theological and religious studies at Drew University, with a special emphasis in sanctification.

Jack Brady's reputation has enabled him to assist with many important initiatives, including one of the first counseling teams at Ground Zero. After serving as a county coroner, Sheriff's chaplain and Project Leadership Director for the Community Foundation of Grant County, Indiana, Inc., he returned to the faculty at Indiana Wesleyan University.

Dawn Brown was a successful businesswoman in the media world, serving as National Implementation Manager for Vivendi-Universal. She currently serves as the Community Development Officer with the Community Foundation of Grant County, Indiana, Inc.

Mike Cline is a senior editor of the *Chronicle-Tribune*, a Paxton Media Group newspaper. His J.D. degree is from the Nashville School of Law, Nashville, TN.

Dr. Heith Drury has influenced hundreds of leaders over the past four decades, including the primary author of this text—now a university colleague. Keith has authored numerous books, for example *The Wonder of Worship: Why We Worship the Way We Do* (Triangle Publishing, 2002), *The Call of a Lifetime* (Wesleyan Publishing House, 2003) and *Holiness for Ordinary People* (the all time best-seller for Wesleyan Publishing House, 1983).

Dr. Judy Huffman spent the first twenty years of her career in counseling. She also has taught around the world in an international travel program. Judy served as Dean of the College of Arts and Sciences at Indiana Wesleyan University before joining the pastoral staff at College Wesleyan Church.

Dr. Jim Laub is the Dean of the MacArthur School of Leadership at Palm Beach Atlantic University. His doctoral research at Florida Atlantic University created the first quantitative assessment tool to measure servant leadership in organizations.

Dr. Steve Lennox is a requested speaker, religion professor, and author of *God With Us: An Introduction to the Old Testament* (Triangle Publishing, 2003) and *Psalms* and *Proverbs* commentaries (Wesleyan Publishing House, 1998 and 1999). He is the Dean of Chapel at Indiana Wesleyan University.

Dr. Jim "Umfundisi" Lo is an author, requested speaker, professor of Intercultural Studies, and a former overseas missionary. He is the author of *Intentional Diversity: Creating Cross-Cultural Ministry Relationships in Your Church* (Wesleyan Publishing House, 2002).

Dr. Bill Millard is the president of Life Discovery, Inc. and the Executive Director of the Center for Life Calling and Leadership at Indiana Wesleyan University (IWU). He teaches leadership and management at IWU and is the author of the *Intrinsic Motivation Assessment Guide & Evaluation (IMAGE)*.

index

notes

notes

notes

notes

notes

notes